# How to Maximise Emot. Wellbeing and Improve I

In this highly practical book, Rona Tutt and Paul Williams explore how schools and other educational settings can provide students with the right environment to support their emotional wellbeing and hence to maximise their learning potential. Encouraging collaboration between education and healthcare professionals, as well as other services, and with families, they show how to develop resilience in young people and provide them with the tools for coping with mental health issues.

Based on a range of practical experiences from many different schools and practitioners, *How to Maximise Emotional Wellbeing and Improve Mental Health* discusses several crucial aspects of wellbeing in educational settings, including:

- Changing attitudes surrounding wellbeing and mental health
- Nurturing resilience, and its application
- Creating a healthy and constructive ethos and environment

Providing extensive case studies, and featuring insightful conversations with school leaders and other professionals, this book will be an essential resource for staff in schools, including those leading in mental health, as well as trainee teachers and anyone with a wider societal concern about mental wellbeing in young people.

**Rona Tutt** has an OBE for her services to special needs education. She is a past president of the National Association of Head Teachers (NAHT) and a fellow of UCL's Centre for Inclusive Education (CIE).

**Paul Williams** has been a head teacher of two London special schools, taking a particular interest in the emotional wellbeing of staff and pupils. Paul has also been a national leader of education (NLE).

# How to Maximise Emotional Wellbeing and Improve Mental Health

The Essential Guide to Establishing a Whole-School Ethos

Rona Tutt and Paul Williams

Routledge
Taylor & Francis Group

LONDON AND NEW YORK

First edition published 2021
by Routledge
2 Park Square, Milton Park, Abingdon, Oxon, OX14 4RN

and by Routledge
52 Vanderbilt Avenue, New York, NY 10017

*Routledge is an imprint of the Taylor & Francis Group, an informa business*

© 2021 Rona Tutt and Paul Williams

The right of Rona Tutt and Paul Williams to be identified as authors
of this work has been asserted by them in accordance with
sections 77 and 78 of the Copyright, Designs and Patents Act 1988.

*British Library Cataloguing-in-Publication Data*
A catalogue record for this book is available from the British Library

*Library of Congress Cataloging-in-Publication Data*
Names: Tutt, Rona, author. | Williams, Paul (Headteacher) author.
Title: How to maximise emotional wellbeing and improve mental
    health : the essential guide to establishing a whole-school ethos /
    Rona Tutt and Paul Williams.
Description: Abingdon, Oxon ; New York, NY : Routledge, 2021. |
    Includes bibliographical references and index. |
Identifiers: LCCN 2020054020 (print) | LCCN 2020054021 (ebook) |
    ISBN 9780367511357 (hardback) | ISBN 9780367511371 (paperback) |
    ISBN 9781003052579 (ebook)
Subjects: LCSH: Students—Mental health. | School improvement
    programs.
Classification: LCC LB3430 .T88 2021 (print) | LCC LB3430 (ebook) |
    DDC 371.7/1—dc23
LC record available at https://lccn.loc.gov/2020054020
LC ebook record available at https://lccn.loc.gov/2020054021

ISBN: 978-0-367-51135-7 (hbk)
ISBN: 978-0-367-51137-1 (pbk)
ISBN: 978-1-003-05257-9 (ebk)

Typeset in Bembo
by Apex CoVantage, LLC

We would like to dedicate this book to all the school, social and NHS staff who support children and young people with their wellbeing and mental health – before, during and after COVID-19.

# Contents

# Abbreviations

| | |
|---|---|
| AAA | Ambitious About Autism |
| ABA | Applied Behaviour Analysis |
| ABI | Acquired Brain Injury |
| ACAMH | Association for Child and Adolescent Mental Health |
| ACE | Adverse Childhood Experiences |
| ADHD | Attention Deficit Hyperactivity Disorder |
| AET | Autism Education Trust |
| AMHS | Adult Mental Health Services |
| AP | Alternative Provision |
| ARP | Additionally Resourced Provision |
| ASD | Autistic Spectrum Disorder |
| AWMSG | All Wales Medicines Strategy Group |
| BAME | Black, Asian and Minority Ethnic |
| BEIS | Department for Business, Energy and Industrial Strategy |
| BESD | Behaviour, Emotional and Social Development |
| CAMHS | Child and Adolescent Mental Health Services |
| CAS | Cognitive Assessment System |
| CBT | Cognitive Behaviour Therapy |
| CCG | Clinical Commissioning Group |
| CD | Conduct Disorder |
| CIC | Community Interest Company |
| CiN | Children in Need |
| CORC | Child Outcomes Research Consortium |
| CPD | Continuing Professional Development |
| CPR | Conditional Positive Regard |
| CQC | Care Quality Commission |
| CWP | Children's Wellbeing Practitioner |
| CYIAPT | Children and Young People's Improving Access to Psychological Therapy |
| CYP | Children and Young People |
| CYPMHS | Children and Young People's Mental Health Services |
| CYPMHT | Children and Young People's Mental Health Taskforce |

| | |
|---|---|
| DBT | Dialectical Behaviour Therapy |
| DfE | Department for Education |
| DHSC | Department of Health and Social Care |
| DoH | Department of Health |
| DSL | Designated Safeguarding Lead |
| EAL | English as an Additional Language |
| EHCP | Education, Health and Care Plan |
| EHRC | Equality and Human Rights Commission |
| EHWBS | Emotional Health and Well Being Service |
| ELA | Emotional Literacy Assessment |
| ELSA | Emotional Literacy Support Assistant |
| EMHP | Education Mental Health Practitioner |
| EOTAS | Education Other Than At School |
| EP | Educational Psychologist |
| ERA | Embedding Restorative Approaches |
| ESC | Education Support Centre |
| EYFS | Early Years Foundation Stage |
| FA | Football Association |
| FAS | Foetal Alcohol Syndrome |
| FE | Further Education |
| FSM | Free School Meals |
| GCSE | General Certificate of Education |
| HLTA | High Level Teaching Assistant |
| HSE | Health and Safety Executive |
| HWB | Health and Wellbeing Board |
| INSET | Inservice Training |
| ITT | Initial Teacher Training |
| KEP | Knowledge Exchange Programme |
| LAC | Looked After Children |
| LADO | Local Authority Designated Officer |
| LGA | Local Government Association |
| LGBT | Lesbian, Gay, Bisexual and Transgender |
| LOtC | Learning Outside the Classroom |
| MAT | Multi Academy Trust |
| MHFA | Mental Health First Aid |
| MHST | Mental Health Support Team |
| MiSP | Mindfulness in School Project |
| MLD | Moderate Learning Difficulties |
| NAHE | National Association for Hospital Education |
| NAHT | National Association of Head Teachers |
| NAPCE | National Association for Pastoral Care in Education |
| NAS | National Autistic Society |
| Nasen | National Association for Special Educational Needs |
| NASENCO | National Award in SEN Coordination |

| | |
|---|---|
| NCS | National Citizen Service |
| NCST | National Citizen Service Trust |
| NEF | New Economics Foundation |
| NHS | National Health Service |
| NICE | National Institute for Health and Care Excellence |
| NIHP | National Institute for Health Protection |
| NLE | National Leader of Education |
| OCD | Obsessive Compulsive Behaviour |
| ODD | Oppositional Defiant Disorder |
| OT | Occupational Therapist |
| PaT | Pets as Therapy |
| PBS | Positive Behaviour Support |
| PCP | Personal Construct Psychology |
| PECS | Picture Exchange Communication System |
| PEP | Personal Education Plan |
| PHE | Public Health England |
| PoS | Programmes of Study |
| PP+ | Pupil Premium Plus |
| PRU | Pupil Referral Unit |
| PSA | Parent Support Adviser |
| PSCHE | Personal, Social, Citizenship and Health Education |
| PSHE | Personal, Social, Health and Economic Education |
| PTSD | Post-Traumatic Stress Disorder |
| p4c | Philosophy forChildren |
| RCADS | Revised Children's Anxiety and Depression Scale |
| RSA | Royal Society of Arts |
| RSC | Regional Schools Commissioner |
| RSE | Relationships and Sex Education |
| RSHE | Relationships, Sex and Health Education |
| SaLT | Speech and Language Therapist |
| SAMH | Scottish Association of Mental Health |
| SDQ | Strengths and Difficulties Questionnaire |
| SEAL | Social and Emotional Aspects of Learning |
| SEBD | Social, Emotional and Behavioural Difficulties |
| SEMH | Social, Emotional and Mental Health Difficulties |
| SENCO | Special Educational Needs Coordinator |
| SEND | Special Educational Needs and Disability |
| SFBT | Solution-Focussed Brief Therapy |
| SHANARRI | Safe, Healthy, Active, Nurtured, Achieving, Respected, Responsible and Included |
| SHARP | Self-Harm Awareness Programme |
| SLA | Service Level Agreement |
| SLCN | Speech, Language and Communication Needs |
| SLE | Specialist Leader of Education |

| | |
|---|---|
| SLT | Senior Leadership Team |
| SMHL | Senior Mental Health Lead |
| SMSC | Spiritual, Moral, Social and Cultural |
| STEAM | Science, Technology, Engineering, Arts and Mathematics |
| SWERL | Supporting Wellbeing, Emotional Resilience and Learning |
| TEACCH | Treatment and Education of Autistic and Communication Handicapped Children |
| Tes | Times Educational Supplement |
| TIS | Therapies in School |
| TISUK | Trauma Informed Schools UK |
| UCL | University College London |
| UKRP | UK Resilience Programme |
| UNCRC | United Nations Convention on the Rights of the Child |
| UNICEF | United Nations International Children's Emergency Fund |
| UPR | Unconditional Positive Regard |
| VSH | Virtual School Head Teacher |
| WE | Whole Education |
| WHO | World Health Organisation |
| WIAT | Weschler Individual Achievement Test |
| YOT | Youth Offending Team |

# Acknowledgements

| | |
|---|---|
| Helen Avey | Head Teacher, Highbury Infant School and Nursery |
| Steven Baker | Executive Head Teacher, Aspire Federation |
| Tim Bowen | Head Teacher, Maple Primary School |
| Chris Britten | Head Teacher, Ysgol y Deri |
| Penny Broadhurst | Assistant Head Teacher, Wellbeing, Prospect School |
| Geri Cameron | Principal Loughshire Education Resource Centre |
| Ben Commins | Executive Head Teacher, Queens Park Primary School |
| Anne Conboy | Head Teacher, Claremont Primary School |
| Claudia Cubbage | Head Teacher, Henry Cort Community College |
| Ruth Davies | Head Teacher, Waunarlwydd School |
| Stephen Deadman | Head Teacher, Leicester Children's Hospital School |
| Siart Deane | Project Manager, Severn Teaching School Alliance |
| Anne Eardley | Head Teacher, Crosshall Junior School |
| Sarah Ellis | Wellbeing and Behaviour Senior Teacher, Oak Grove College |
| Timothy Ellis | Head Teacher, Leamington LAMP |
| Robert Gasson | Chief Executive, Wave MAT |
| Dr Janice Howkins | Head Teacher, Bentley Wood School |
| Tracy Jennings | Deputy Head Teacher, St Elizabeth Catholic School |
| Issy Jerrard | Wellbeing Lead, Forest Oak School |
| Shanti Johnson | Deputy Head Teacher, Maple Primary School |
| Lyndsy Killip | Head of School, Queens Park Primary School |
| Antonia McConnell-Smith | Assistant Head Teacher Inclusion, Whitehill Junior School and Inclusion Coordinator Highbury Infant School and Nursery |

| | |
|---|---|
| Carolyn McKay | Education Mental Health Practitioner |
| Marijke Miles | Head Teacher, Baycroft School |
| Steve Mills | Head Teacher, Whitehill Junior School |
| Amanda Mordey | Principal, Forest Oak School |
| Andrew O'Sullivan | Head Teacher, Durham Johnston School |
| Lorraine Petersen | Education Consultant |
| Phillip Potter | Head Teacher, Oak Grove College |
| Kathryn Pugh | Head Teacher, The St Marylebone C. of E. School |
| Dr Amelia Roberts | Vice Dean, Enterprise, University College London |
| Matthew Sartin | Head Teacher, Springhallow School |
| Paul Scales | Principal, Church Lawton School |
| Lindsey Shaw | Head Teacher, Belmont School |
| Nicky Sutton | Wellbeing Lead, St Francis School |
| Paul Thomson | Head Teacher, Baltasound Junior High School |
| Sarah Watson | Deputy Head Teacher, Furze Down School |
| Nick Weaver | Assistant Head Teacher Inclusion, Durham Johnston School |

# Foreword: from recovery to resilience

The book is not only timely, it is vital and necessary. With its core purpose of encouraging the process of building emotional resilience in our Children and Young People (CYP), the focus on good practice in Mental Health and Emotional Wellbeing is welcome.

Conceived pre-pandemic, with a gestation during the pandemic period, this book is 'born' into a post-pandemic world where society is assessing the 'cost' not just in financial terms, but the cost to its people in terms of their mental health and wellbeing.

We have seen a rapid erosion in the mental health of our CYP since the lockdown of March 2020. The Institute of Fiscal Studies has reported an 8.7% decline. National Health Service (NHS) monitoring is observing spikes in self-harm and eating disorders. These are occurring in children younger than previously known. I have personally watched a young girl of 11, who before March 2020 was perfectly healthy, spiral into an eating disorder that by September was diagnosed as anorexic. Eventually she refused even a sip of water and was admitted to hospital for 're-feeding'. By October she entered a specialist NHS residential facility.

We have to ask why a much-loved child from a stable family would deteriorate so rapidly with such pervasive, life-threatening mental ill health? The loss of control this girl experienced over her own life is mirrored in the lives of many children, not in such an extreme form perhaps, but it is, for them, a vivid reality. Action, support and intervention is crucial, which is why the contents of this book are so welcomed.

Our quest in schools must be to restore and rejuvenate the emotional wellbeing of all of our children. No child can have escaped unscathed from the terror of this pandemic which stalked our communities, taking many, many lives. Therefore, our curriculum journey has to be one of re-building our children's emotional resilience through dynamic innovation and creative learning experiences, starting, as HMCI Amanda Spielman (2020) says, 'where each child is at'. She goes on to say 'that many children are angry at the world'. They deserve an explanation of what is coronavirus, a pandemic, etc. It is unthinkable that any child should be emotionally scarred for life by the events of the pandemic period.

In the Recovery Curriculum (Carpenter and Carpenter, 2020), we identified five losses – routine, structure, friendship, opportunity and freedom. The impact of these losses can have serious consequences on the life of a child, giving rise to anxiety, a bereavement response, attachment issues – all of which are forms of trauma and can have a life disorientating impact. As the Royal College of Paediatricians & Child Health (2020) reported:

> there is a real risk that current health inequalities will widen (and) vulnerable children will slip through the net.

There is much adversity in our world resulting from the global pandemic. This adversity has permeated our children's lives and more than ever we, as teachers, need to have a clear grasp on the implications of adverse childhood experiences (ACE). In this respect the new definition offered by MindEd (2020) is insightful:

> A child whose mind and body are overly stressed and in fight, flight or freeze mode is not open for learning.
>
> ACEs have short and long term negative life changing consequences across education, health, care, criminal justice and later employment and life expectancy outcomes.

The curriculum currently needs to reflect the lived experience of the child. So, to reflect the MindEd statement in a child's words, when trialling pictures for two children's stories (Carpenter et al., 2020) recently in a primary school, one Year 5 child described lockdown as 'locked-in'. A slip of the tongue, but not an inaccurate description. For many children the lockdown period and periods of self-isolation must have felt as if they were 'locked-in', deprived of their freedom to see friends, play outdoors and breathe fresh air. Lockdown is not a natural childhood state, and the constraint and restraint it has imposed on children has felt alien to them, generating feelings of frustration, anxiety, worry and more. As the lockdown progressed and the turmoil of the pandemic raged, many children and young people felt that their hopes for the future were being dashed. And hope is the gift of childhood.

Modern life has been chipping away at children's happiness over time. *The Good Childhood Report* (2020) finds that this toxic trend has continued. They call on the government to put children's wellbeing at the centre of the recovery from coronavirus process. The global pandemic has seriously affected children's happiness due to the lack of choice they have had.

Relationships are at the heart of that process of recovery and, indeed, is the first of the '5 Levers' articulated in the Recovery Curriculum (op. cit.). Before we can hope to return to a full curriculum we must re-calibrate children's learning, including the state of their mental health which, if poor, will ultimately undermine their potential attainment and achievement. This book gives powerful examples of how this process is already happening in our schools. We can marshal this creative thinking and innovative practice, and design learning pathways which invite children to re-join their school communities as active participants, reconnecting with friends and teachers.

Compassionate leadership will be key to this process and to re-establishing the wellbeing of the whole-school community. Kindness matters, too. At a time when the future is uncertain and we feel disconnected, our mental health and wellbeing frail and fragile, the smallest act of kindness can have the biggest effect.

The NHS has acknowledged that "having a nurturing and compassionate approach in the classroom that underpins learning, will be helpful in re-generating relationships" (Chitsabesan, 2020). Schools are generating such responses, as the rich examples in this book powerfully illustrate.

This book is a beacon that will shine a bright light through the mayhem of mental health needs in our children and young people, created by the global pandemic, enabling teachers to restore our children to their rightful state of successful learner, for their emotional wellbeing to flourish, and for education once more to be a dignifying process for all children.

*Barry Carpenter, CBE*

*Professor of Mental Health in Education,*
*Oxford Brookes University*
*October 2020*

## References

Carpenter, B., and Carpenter, M. J. (2020) *The Recovery Curriculum: Loss and Life for Our Children and Schools in the Pandemic.* Think Piece. Available from www.recoverycurriculum.org.uk

Carpenter, B., Erskine, A., and Hawkes, J. (2020) *Lenny and Lily in Lockdown: Lenny and Lily Return to School.* Available from www.booksbeyondwords.co.uk

Children's Society (2020) *The Good Childhood Report: Summer Update.* Available from www.childrenssociety.org.uk

Chitsabesan, P. (2020) *Impact of Covid-19 on Children and Young People's Mental Health.* Lecture Given to the DfE Online Mental Health Conference, 9th July.

MindEd (2020) *Adverse Childhood Experiences Programme.* Available from www.minded.org.uk/component/details/653614

Royal College of Paediatricians & Child Health (2020) *Restoring Children's Health Services, Covid-19, and Winter Planning: Position Statement.* RCPCH, London.

Spielman, A. (2020) *Rebuilding.* An Interview with BBC Radio 4 'Today' Programme, 6th July.

# Chapter 1

# Changing attitudes in changing times

This book was written during a year that straddled the time before COVID-19 had hit countries across the globe and the time when the devastating ramifications of the pandemic were beginning to emerge. The Secretary-General of the United Nations, António Guterres, described the event as the most challenging crisis since World War Two. The uncertain future for major industries and local businesses alike are stark and the effects of rising unemployment threatens to blight too many lives, as a world we had come to rely on disappeared almost overnight. The visible signs of how the world had changed were all too obvious, but what may have been less apparent were the lasting effects on people's mental health and wellbeing, as families and friends had long periods when they were unable to meet to socialise, to celebrate, or even to mourn together.

In his foreword to a report in July 2020, Mark Russell, Chief Executive of The Children's Society, said there had been a decline in children's wellbeing since well before the pandemic, with children's happiness with their lives being at its lowest since 2009/10. However, he went on to say:

> But there is hope. While children are feeling the impacts now of the coronavirus and the lockdown measures, there is still a sense of optimism for their future. Children told us that through these difficult times they have enjoyed having a time to reflect, to learn new hobbies or restart old ones and have found gratitude for things in their life pre-lockdown.
>
> (2020: 2)

Similar conclusions were reached by Anne Longfield, the Children's Commissioner for England. In a report a couple of months later, she began by saying that some families had said they had enjoyed being able to spend more time together, when children were out of school and parents were having to work from home. She commented, too, on the dedication and commitment of many teachers, social workers and other professionals during this time. However, she pointed out that even before the pandemic, there were 2.2 million children in England living in households affected by domestic abuse, parental drug and/or alcohol dependency and severe parental mental health issues (Children's Commissioner for England, 2020).

It remains to be seen what the long-term effects of COVID-19 will be on the mental health and wellbeing of people of all ages. But what is clear is that the current crisis will throw a spotlight on emotional wellbeing and on the part schools and other educational settings can play in improving the mental health of the nation.

## Recognising the importance of mental health

Well before the advent of the coronavirus, there had been a shift towards recognising the importance of emotional wellbeing, but there is still some distance to go before people are as open and well informed about their mental wellbeing as they are about their physical health – yet the two are closely intertwined. In addition, societal changes from well before the virus have made it harder for people of all ages to remain resilient. Instead of an extended family of grandparents, cousins and other family members living nearby, families may be scattered across the country and, increasingly, across the globe, leaving the nuclear family less cushioned without the wider family's support to draw on.

Another growing pressure has been the rise in social media, leading to less face-to-face contact and more time spent shut off from engaging with the real world. An increase in indoor activity has been noted along with a decrease in outdoor pursuits, which is one of the areas where physical and mental health merge. Meanwhile a digital divide has opened up between households equipped to access online education, information and advice, and those whose lack of technology leaves them further behind.

An unintended consequence of the reliance on social media has been a rise in bullying and other forms of unacceptable behaviour, which is affecting people of all ages. Bullies have always existed, but now that it is possible to attack or belittle people while hiding behind a screen of anonymity, it has become more invidious, more damaging and more extreme. In June 2019, as part of an inquiry into funding in Northern Ireland, the Northern Ireland Affairs Committee in Westminster heard from Geri Cameron, Principal of Loughshore Education Centre in Belfast. Geri said that a strategy for protecting teachers and their wellbeing is sorely needed, saying:

> I can't imagine any other situation where a school principal could be hounded, stalked and vilified on social media and held up for public ridicule with no consequence.

(There is more about bullying in Chapter 4, where attention is paid both to the bully and to the bullied.)

Responding to a question about the scale of support for pupils with mental health problems Geri added that:

There isn't a school in Northern Ireland at the moment which isn't feeling the effects of the challenges of dealing with children and young people who have mental ill-health.

The same would apply to other parts of the UK as well. However, as this book shows, there are some amazing examples of what schools and other settings are doing to support young learners' mental health, and if the intentions of the 2017 Green Paper on Mental Health (DoH and DfE, 2017) finally come to fruition – in combination with other approaches outlined in this book and elsewhere – the future could be much more promising than the past, once the battle with the coronavirus recedes.

Turning to further education (FE) colleges in January 2020, the Times Educational Supplement (tes) (which reaches schools in more than 100 countries and has offices in England, Hong Kong, Sydney and Dubai), did a survey of 142 FE colleges. An article headed: 'The "tsunami" of mental health need' summed up its findings:

- 17,500 students were seeing a counsellor or accessing mental health support regularly
- 914 had a dedicated mental health responsibility, which had more than doubled in three years
- More than 120 of the colleges ran a counselling service for students
- The number of staff who had received some form of mental health awareness training had increased by over 700% in the same three-year period (Tes, 2020)

The long-standing and rising concern about young learners' mental wellbeing has resulted in a more concerted effort to address the issue and, as well as mental health charities and other organisations rising to the challenge, their voices have been added to by a growing number of figures in the public eye – from royalty to film stars and from footballers to TV pundits.

## Opening up the conversation

Not only is this a significant step forward, but it has also been part of a growing trend for organisations to work collaboratively with others in the field. While there are so many developments that it is not possible to find the space to cover them all, here are some examples of the work that has been going on in recent years:

- The Duke and Duchess of Cambridge have made mental health one of their main areas of charity work and launched the 'Heads Together' campaign to tackle stigma
- A legacy of 'Heads Together' was the setting up of the 'Mentally Healthy Schools' website (www.mentallyhealthyschools.org.uk/), in conjunction

with The Anna Freud Centre, Place2Be and YoungMinds, giving school and college staff access to quality-assured resources, advice and information. From 2020, the range of resources has widened to include the whole of the UK

- 'Heads Together' and the Football Association (FA) teamed up for the 'Heads Up' campaign to drive home the message to football fans of all ages
- In 2019 'Mental Health Innovations' launched its first digital programme with the introduction of 'Shout', which is a free 24/7 text messaging service for people needing immediate support

During Mental Health Awareness Week 2019, an English TV presenting duo, Anthony McPartlin and Declan Donnelly, commonly known as Ant and Dec, used one of their popular television shows to launch a Mental Wellness campaign, 'Britain Get Talking', supported by the mental health charities Mind, YoungMinds, and the Scottish Association for Mental Health (SAMH). Every year, there is a Mental Health Awareness week in the UK.

---

**Information point   Mental Health Awareness Week**

Mental Health Awareness Week has been run by the Mental Health Foundation since 2001.

It is a week in May every year devoted to raising the awareness of mental health and inspire action to promote the message of good mental health for all.

Schools, businesses, community groups and people in their own homes host events to raise money for the Mental Health Foundation, which produces free resources for the occasion.

The week is widely advertised by other mental health charities, such as Mind, Time to Change, Healthwatch, Anxiety UK, Rethink Mental Illness, Shout, Every Mind Matters, etc.

---

(There is further information about these charities and their campaigns in Chapter 7.)

## Competing and conflicting agendas

Despite a more welcoming environment and a greater recognition of the need to nurture wellbeing in people of all ages, the efforts of schools to offer a rounded education has not always been enough to counteract successive governments' unhealthy obsession with measuring a school's success purely in terms of tracking academic progress. Pupils' results are used to hold schools accountable, as if the complex work of schools can be summed up in a few bald statistics, while a fleeting visit by Ofsted inspectors can impact how schools are viewed by the public and affect how staff and pupils feel about themselves.

The time, money and energy that has gone into devising baselines for measuring children's readiness for learning the minute they arrive in their reception classroom; the diktats about how pupils should be taught to read and write; and the insistence on priority being given to certain GCSE subjects at the expense of The Arts does not help to inspire and motivate pupils. FE colleges have a particular problem in trying to enthuse their students with a love of learning when they are required to re-sit their English and maths, carrying with them unsuccessful attempts at school to reach the required standard into the next stage of their education. While it is a welcome step that there is now a greater focus on wellbeing, it might not have been as necessary if teachers had been trusted to teach and children had been treated as unique individuals with their own interests, aptitudes and abilities.

In 2017, YoungMinds began its 'Wise Up' campaign which calls on the government to rebalance the education system to make the wellbeing of students as important as academic achievement. In pressing its case, it points out that three children in every classroom are likely to have a diagnosable mental disorder and 90% of school leaders have reported an increase in the last five years in the number of students experiencing anxiety, stress, low mood or depression.

Similarly, an emphasis on disciplining pupils and controlling 'bad' behaviour, rather than recognising behaviour as a form of communication, has been less than helpful. The tide is turning, but the arguments still rumble on. It was a hopeful sign when Department for Education (DfE) guidance went from talking about 'behaviour and discipline in schools' (DfE, 2014) to giving guidance on 'mental health and behaviour in schools', with the latter recognising that a pupil's behaviour may be caused by mental health issues. This guidance also suggests that, while there is no requirement to have a separate Mental Health and Wellbeing policy, a range of other policies should show how the topic is being covered. (An example of a Positive Mental Health policy is given in Chapter 3 and case studies of different ways of covering mental health in the curriculum are discussed in Chapter 5.)

## The significance of the change from BESD to SEMH

Another major step in the right direction was when the current special educational needs and disabilities (SEND) Code of Practice (DfE, 2015) adjusted one of the four broad areas of need from the previous version. Retained were:

- Communication and interaction
- Cognition and learning
- Sensory and/or physical needs

However, the other category of:

- Behaviour, emotional and social development (BESD) was changed to social, emotional and mental health difficulties (SEMH)

This meant that the word 'behaviour' was dropped altogether and 'mental health' was mentioned instead. The Code of Practice explains that children and young people may experience a wide range of social and emotional difficulties, from the isolated or withdrawn child to the one who displays disturbed and disturbing behaviour.

There is no suggestion, here or elsewhere, that teachers should be able to diagnose mental health conditions, but they should be aware that some behaviours may be the result of a pupil having a mental health issue. Nor is there a suggestion that the Special Education Needs Co-ordinator (SENCO) should automatically be responsible for pupils with mental health needs, simply because BESD has changed to SEMH. Although there is some overlap, and children with SEND are more likely than those who do not have SEND to develop mental health issues, having strategic oversight of mental health and emotional wellbeing in the school is seen as a significant role. (There are further discussions about this in Chapters 2 and 3.)

## Defining the terminology

One of the changes that has emerged as children and young people's wellbeing has gained a higher profile has been the use of descriptions, such as mental health, mental wellbeing, wellbeing and emotional wellbeing. While there seems to be no agreed definition for some of these terms, or a consensus about how far they overlap, there is a common thread running through many of the definitions. Starting with the meaning of 'wellbeing', which The Children's Society report mentioned earlier, points out that wellbeing can be used in a number of ways:

> Wellbeing is a commonly used term which, in everyday life, can refer to a range of things including happiness, not being ill, or having enough money. Not surprisingly, this array of definitions is also reflected in the way that wellbeing is measured.
>
> (2020: 9)

A definition clarifying the relationship between mental health and wellbeing comes from the World Health Organisation (WHO). This definition is widely accepted and frequently quoted:

> Mental health is defined as a state of wellbeing in which every individual recognises his or her own potential, can cope with the normal stresses of

life, can work productively and fruitfully, and is able to make a contribution to his or her own community.

(2014)

On its website, the Mental Health Foundation builds on the WHO definition as follows:

> A positive sense of wellbeing (which) enables an individual to be able to function in society and meet the demands of everyday life; people in good mental health have the ability to recover effectively from illness, change or misfortune.

The last part of this definition adds the idea that people who are in this positive state are in a position to be resilient and recover from setbacks. (There is more about resilience in Chapter 4.)

The terms 'emotional wellbeing' and 'mental health' can be used interchangeably or together. As the focus in this book is on the emotional development and wellbeing of young people so that they will have good mental health, this is the approach that is taken and is reflected in the book's title. When discussing models of emotional development, a book edited by Colley and Cooper (2017) sheds light on the importance of emotional development:

> For a significant minority of children in your classroom, the inability to recognise their own emotional states or regulate their impulses will be undermining both their learning and their relationships in school. Locked in stages of emotional development that are now out of step with their chronological age, these children will be battling to manage emotions and feelings that might include mistrust, aggression, disdain, anxiety and shame.

(2017: 27)

## Achieving wellbeing

In a white paper in 1999, a labour government set out an action plan for healthier living. This included a section on the importance of mental health for everyone which had steps for enhancing emotional wellbeing. These were:

- Keeping in touch with family and friends
- Keeping involved in the community
- Making time for relaxation
- Making time for physical activity
- Asking for help and talking about problems

(H.M. Government, 1999)

It is interesting to see how these steps relate to what has become known as the NHS's 'Five steps to mental wellbeing'.

In response to the government's request for a succinct message about how to improve wellbeing that might be as catchy as the 'Five fruit and vegetables a day' message, the New Economics Foundation (NEF, 2011) arrived at the 'Five ways to mental wellbeing', which, in turn, led to the NHS version published in 2008 and updated in 2020, when the phrase was changed to 'Five *steps* to mental wellbeing' (NHS, 2008). An even more succinct version appears on the website of Mind (www.mind.org.uk/), with the same ideas in a slightly different order.

| *NHS* | *Mind* |
|---|---|
| 1. Connect with other people | 1. Connect |
| 2. Be physically active | 2. Be active |
| 3. Learn new skills | 3. Take notice |
| 4. Give to others | 4. Learn |
| 5. Pay attention to the present moment (mindfulness) | 5. Give |

These steps or ways to wellbeing have been well researched. They have achieved the original aim of making an impact and are used across the services. The following two case studies are of schools that have embedded these ideas very firmly in their settings.

### Case study of St Francis C. of E. Primary School

St Francis C. of E. Primary School in Cornwall has made mental health and wellbeing a priority. The school has explained wellbeing as follows:

> Wellbeing is when you feel good and enjoy your day-to-day life. The things that we do and the way that we think affects our wellbeing and there are five ways that can help boost this. Each of these actions makes a positive difference to how we feel, being aware of and combining these will make a difference.

Suggestions are made as to the actions that might be taken to fulfil each of the five ways:

| 1 | *Connect* | With your friends, family, neighbours and people at work. Have a conversation, pass the time of day, make time for that chat |
| 2 | *Be active* | Find a physical activity that you enjoy, go for a walk, try gardening |
| 3 | *Take notice* | Take the time to look at the day, the changing seasons; savour the moment |

4   *Keep learning*   Try something new whether it's making a new recipe, fixing your bike or even signing up for a course

5   *Give*   Smile, do something nice for a friend or neighbour, make some time for others

## Case study   St Francis C. of E. Primary School, Falmouth

St Francis is a two-form entry school in the centre of Falmouth. It is part of the Kernow Learning Multi-Academy Trust (MAT), which has a number of schools in south-west England. The head teacher is Hannah Stevens.

In order to raise pupils' awareness of wellbeing, the school decided to develop an initiative based on the NHS 'Five steps to mental wellbeing'. Wellbeing Champions were created from amongst the pupils, each one being responsible for one of the five ways and each having five pupils on their team. Pupils who are above reception age can put themselves forward for these roles. The only help from staff comes from a sixth team which provides administrative support to the other teams.

To date, the teams have been hard at work and have developed the following activities:

| | |
|---|---|
| *Connect Team* | Running a 'Chatters Matters' club; being Gate Greeters |
| *Take Notice Team* | Running a yoga club |
| *Give Team* | Focusing on giving out friendship tokens |
| *Keep Learning Team* | Running a 'Reading Shed' |
| *Be Active Team* | Running team games at lunchtime |
| *Admin Team* | Delivering friendship postcards and supporting the teams |

The Wellbeing Champions and their teams have the responsibility of developing new ideas and encouraging other pupils to join in with the activities. This is a very practical way of helping all pupils to understand the concept of wellbeing and to be actively involved in improving their own wellbeing, as well as contributing to the wellbeing of those around them.

Now that these teams have become well established, the school hopes to create a 'Parents five ways to wellbeing group'.

As another example of the school's commitment to the mental health and wellbeing of its pupils, the school is a trauma informed school (TIS) and five members of staff have been trained as TIS practitioners. This means that they know how to support pupils who have suffered from trauma of some kind, as well as pupils whose troubled behaviour may be due to underlying mental health issues. Nicky Sutton, a member of the Senior Leadership Team (SLT), is the Pastoral Lead, the Wellbeing and TIS Lead and the PSHE Co-ordinator.

---

### Information point   Trauma informed schools (TIS)

Trauma informed schools (TIS) are recognised by TISUK, whose objective is to bring about a whole-school or organisational cultural shift where the wellbeing of all is the highest priority. TISUK believes that for schools to become mentally healthy places for all, the value of wellbeing has to be recognised and starts at the very top, not just in schools and colleges, but in organisations such as DfE, Ofsted and the Regional Schools Commissioners (RSCs) who are responsible for standards in academies. This means that there has to be a balance between outcomes as measured by test scores and emotional wellbeing.

TISUK runs 4 awards:

Mentally Healthy School Award    Mental Health Organisation Award
Trauma and Mental Health Informed School Award
Trauma and Mental Health Informed Organisation Award

---

### Case study of Forest Oak and Merstone Schools

Amanda Mordey is the Executive Principal of two special schools in Solihull: Merstone School for pupils aged 2 to 19 who have severe and complex learning difficulties and Forest Oak School for pupils aged 4 to 18 who have moderate learning difficulties (MLD). Both schools are located on the same site. In 2014, Issy Jerrard, Wellbeing Lead at Forest Oak, worked with the Solihull Advisory Team on a research project which resulted in the SMILE (**S**ocialise, **M**ove, **I**nterest, **L**earn, **E**ngage) approach. This is an ethos-based approach to promoting positive mental health and wellbeing for children with SEND.

The school took the NHS 'Five steps to wellbeing' approach and adapted the words, so they were easier for the pupils to understand and remember:

| NHS | Forest Oak |
|-----|------------|
| Connect with other people | **Socialise** and connect with others |
| Be physically active | **Move** and get active |
| Pay attention to the present moment | **Interest** . . . notice things |
| Learning new skills | **Learn** and keep learning |
| Give to others | **Engage** in something big and give to others |

Having found this approach was very successful in their own schools, Amanda and Issy were keen to find out how it might work elsewhere. A two-year evidence-based trial of SMILE was commissioned across five primary and five special schools. Although the final report has yet to be published, the ten schools involved say they have already seen a significant shift in culture and that SMILE has enabled them to make sure that the wellbeing of the whole-school community takes centre stage. The principles behind this approach are:

1   Building emotional resilience for all – children, staff and the whole-school community
2   Promoting good mental health that leads to good life outcomes
3   Listening to each other
4   Care, concern and respect for everyone
5   Kindness and gratitude

## Case study    Forest Oak and Merstone Schools – Solihull

Both these schools have a focus on wellbeing and see the SMILE approach as helping staff and students to become 'Architects of their own emotional health and wellbeing'.

After the keywords making up the acronym 'SMILE' had been agreed, a list of relevant activities to go with each one was compiled and illustrated with photos and cartoons:

| | |
|---|---|
| Socialise | Talk, listen, be a friend, spend time with family, say hello and chat |
| Move | Walk, dance, skip, play a sport, exercise how you like |
| Interest | Relax, use your senses, be aware of your feelings, recognise things around you, focus on your breathing |
| Learn | Read a book, try a craft, join a club, try something new, set school and work goals |
| Engage | Smile, be kind, say thank you, offer to help, include others, volunteer |

Now that the approach has become embedded, it has helped pupils – and the staff – to identify coping strategies and to be able to do something positive when they are stressed or anxious, rather than feeling negative. One development has been staff taking up a new interest and learning alongside the children. This has the benefit of showing the pupils that they are better at some activities than their teachers, which does wonders for their self-esteem.

The schools have 'Being Kind' tokens which are placed in boxes, one for pupils and one for staff. Both pupils and staff can nominate a member of staff for a token. Once a week, a token is pulled out at random and a prize awarded to a lucky winner from each box.

Butterfly Print has worked in close collaboration with Forest Oak's Wellbeing Lead, Issy Jerrard, to create a range of resources to support the SMILE wellbeing approach. These feature illustrations from a Y11 pupil at the school. Recently, Amanda, Issy and staff have worked to launch SMILE for wider use through Barry Carpenter's Recovery Curriculum. (Further details are given in Chapter 7 of both the Recovery Curriculum and Butterfly Print's resources.)

## Mental health conditions and developmental disorders

Developmental disorders, which are also called neurodevelopmental disorders, appear at birth or during early childhood, although they may not be diagnosed until later. They are lifelong conditions and so cannot be cured as such, although they can certainly be ameliorated. Education can make a huge difference to how some of these pupils develop.

Mental illnesses or disorders, on the other hand, can occur at any age and will last for varying lengths of time. They are treatable, often with medication, therapy or a combination of both. They can be chronic, temporary or recur in episodes. They are health conditions that involve changes in mood, emotion, thinking and behaviour. They are likely to affect a person's perceptions and thought processes, and so will impact on their ability to function and to relate to others. Some people may have multiple conditions, including combinations of developmental disorders and mental illnesses.

While mental illness and developmental disorders have key differences, they also have some similarities. Both are diagnosed and treated by health professionals, including therapists, psychologists and psychiatrists. Both mental illness and developmental disorders occur in people of all ethnic, racial and economic groups.

## Autism

Autism is mentioned here because it is sometimes described as a mental health condition, when it is, in fact, a lifelong neurodevelopmental disorder. It affects how the person sees the world around them, how they communicate and how they relate to other people. The behaviour of autistic people can appear unusual, which may arise from trying to cope with a situation they do not fully understand. Attention deficit hyperactivity disorder (ADHD) and autism are two well-known developmental disorders that are increasingly being diagnosed together.

There has been a belated recognition that girls who have autism present differently from boys and may not stand out in the same way. They may cope with primary education by copying their peers and masking their difficulties, but as they enter adolescence, the combination of hitting puberty and the strain of not feeling able to be themselves can result in mental health difficulties, particularly if their autism goes unrecognised. (References are given at the end of this chapter to two recent publications on autism and girls.)

## Identifying mental health issues

It is often said that a little knowledge is a dangerous thing, and it is certainly the case that the role of those who work in education – rather than the health services – is not to diagnose mental health conditions but to know enough to be able to spot when someone may need help. One of the problems is that unlike physical illness, which can often be identified by obvious symptoms such as a fever, a rash or, if necessary, an X-ray, with mental health conditions it can be harder to tell when action needs to be taken. According to Satchwell-Hirst (2017), when writing about 'neuroscience and emotional development in the classroom', the most common mental health problems in childhood and adolescence are depression and anxiety, both of which have wide ranges of severity.

Any of us may feel worried, scared or tense in certain situations, but an anxiety disorder means there is such a pervasive sense of anxiety and fear that it prevents a person's ability to live life as fully as they would wish. Similarly with depression, there are times of sadness in all our lives, but when there is a long-lasting feeling of low mood that makes us lose interest in the everyday activities of life, saps our energy and removes any feeling of pleasure, it becomes a clinical condition. These conditions can affect both physical and mental health showing how closely the two are intertwined and proving again how unhelpful it is to be less open about one than the other.

As has been stressed before, there is absolutely no intention to turn educational professionals into experts in identifying specific mental health concerns, but, as it is known that unhappy children are not in a good state to learn, being concerned about their students' emotional wellbeing is part of the role of those who work in educational settings. The Mental Health Foundation gives general signs to look out for in people of all ages:

- Long-lasting sadness or irritability
- Extremely high and low moods
- Excessive fear, worry or anxiety

- Social withdrawal
- Dramatic changes in eating or sleeping habits

The Mental Health Foundation says that its focus is on prevention, which, when it can be achieved, might be seen as a stage before early intervention.

In the DfE guidance on mental health referred to earlier, it says that:

> Where children experience a range of emotional and behavioural problems that are outside the normal range for their age, they might be described as experiencing mental health problems or disorders.
>
> (2018: para 3.2)

The DfE suggests that there are two key elements to identifying pupils who are at risk of mental health problems, namely:

1   Effective use of data to determine changes in attendance, attainment or behaviour
2   An effective pastoral system, where at least one member of the staff knows every pupil well and has had additional training as to when a child's behaviour might suggest the need to seek its cause

In fact, many schools, well before the Green Paper on Mental Health (and as outlined in the next chapter), had been using these and other ways of identifying pupils. With reference to gathering data, some schools use well-known questionnaires, such as the Boxall Profile Questionnaire and the Strengths and Difficulties Questionnaire (SDQ). Both rely on observation, something teachers are generally very good at, as they notice how their pupils are feeling and if their behaviour changes.

---

### Information point   The Boxall Profile Questionnaire

The Boxall Profile is a resource for assessing children and young people's social, emotional and behavioural development. It helps with:

- Early identification and assessment
- Target setting an intervention
- Tracking progress

More recently, there is now The Boxall Profile Online, which has two Boxall Profile Tests: one for nursery and primary-aged children and one for secondary school students (https://new.boxallprofile.org/).

---

**Information point    The Strengths and Difficulties Questionnaire (SDQ)**

The SDQ is an emotional and behavioural screening questionnaire for children and young people between the ages of 2 and 17. It was developed by a UK child psychiatrist in 1997.

The 25 items in the SDQ comprise five scales of five items each. The scales include:

- Emotional symptoms subscale
- Conduct problems subscale
- Hyperactivity/inattention subscale
- Peer relationships problem subscale
- Prosocial behaviour subscale

Other schools have used the 'Thrive' online programme for assessing pupils' needs; the Social and Emotional Aspects of Learning (SEAL) questionnaires; or have designed their own questionnaires for pupils, staff or both. (Thrive online and SEAL are explained more fully in later chapters.)

The second point the DfE makes is about having an effective pastoral system; this is discussed in Chapter 5.

At this point it may be worth noting that having a key person in the life of a young learner is often crucial. The importance of knowing that someone cares enough to notice when they are going through a tough time, or who they can turn to for support and understanding, can make all the difference. This is something that smaller establishments, such as special schools or alternative provision, can provide more easily. But with the plan to have a strategic lead for mental health in every school, as well as a number of staff who have been trained at various levels in this area, the future looks promising for those who may need something beyond that which has previously been provided for the majority.

### Case study of the Aspire Schools Federation

To round off this chapter, there is a case study of a federation of two SEMH schools, where the executive head teacher, Steven Baker, has considerable experience regarding the effects of recognising behaviour as a form of communication. Following the case study, there is a conversation with Steven, whose work with Dr Alice Jones, Senior Lecturer at Goldsmiths University of London, has been instrumental in moving his schools forward. When Steven explained to her that punishments didn't seem to work, she pointed out that:

> Punishment is ineffectual for some pupils who have an "inhibited fear response" and do not make an association between poor behaviour and adverse

consequences, while others simply do not care. . . . Punishment doesn't really work for those kids, as it doesn't affect their brains in the same way.

Alice explained that rewards often do work, provided there is a range of different rewards to appeal to pupils. But, in this case, the spotlight should be off the poor behaviour and firmly on the behaviours the school wants to see. As a result, Steven explains, he has replaced punishment with compassion.

## Case study   The Aspire Schools Federation, The Wirral

The Aspire Schools Federation is made up of two schools: Gilbrook School, a primary school for 60 pupils and Kilgarth School, a secondary school for 55 boys aged between 11 and 16. Both schools are for pupils whose EHCPs specify that they have SEMH. This includes pupils whose complex needs may include ADHD, autism, foetal alcohol syndrome (FAS), attachment disorder and MLD. The whole ethos of both schools is based on care, responsibility and mutual respect. The children are encouraged to manage and overcome their difficulties within a climate that promotes curiosity and learning. The schools have high expectations of what they will achieve academically, morally and socially so that they will be able to become active and responsible members of society.

The head teacher of Gilbrook School, Kirsten Brown, says that the core ethos is 'Together we can achieve' and this underpins a belief that to succeed there needs to be a cohesive approach that involves families and other agencies. The high expectations for pupils are linked to their personal aspirations. The staff aim to provide a caring, nurturing environment that allows pupils to access, enjoy and make progress on their educational journey, while encouraging them to show an interest in, and care for, others. Kirsten's 'Welcome' on the school's website is directed at the pupils who may be apprehensive about moving schools and is written in a language and a style they can relate to, rather than a more typical introduction aimed at parents and carers.

The head teacher of Kilgarth School, Ms J. Westlake, runs a school in an area of deprivation with little outside space. Nevertheless, positive relationships and a non-confrontational approach prevent the pupils from getting caught in a downward spiral. A rewards-based modification programme encourages responsibility. Staff believe that one of the most important rewards is praise, provided that, at the same time as praising the pupil, the reason why they are being praised is made explicit. Another reward is to spend time with the school's therapy dog, which also provides support for pupils at times of emotional pressure.

Steven sees his pupils as being given a second chance and he and the staff do everything they can to help them make the most of their education so that they can turn a feeling of failure into a successful educational experience before they leave.

### In conversation with Steven Baker

**What do you think about the change from BESD to SEMH?**
It has made a difference and been helpful in focusing minds on the causes of a young person's behaviour rather than concentrating on the behaviour itself.

**Have you noticed a difference in the type of pupils you have now compared to a few years ago?**
Yes, today's pupils have a wider range of needs and are more complex, with many having more than one condition.

**How did the Aspire Schools Federation come about? Are Gilbrook and Kilgarth Schools run on similar lines?**
The Federation happened about five years ago when I had been head teacher of Kilgarth for some years. Gilbrook is a similar school for primary-aged children and needed a head. I took the opportunity to lead a Federation, as I'm keen to have a greater influence on how we address these children's needs. The schools are run on similar lines apart from being for different age groups. Gilbrook has more outdoor space and has a farm, which started with a guinea pig. When we realised how much the children responded to having an animal around, we built it up to the collection of animals we have today, which includes dogs, rabbits, goats, sheep and a micro pig which is very large! I'm keen to develop the use of outdoor space to promote positive mental health and resilience in our pupils.

**What happens when pupils at Gilbrook reach secondary age?**
When pupils leave Gilbrook, they may be ready to return to a mainstream environment, move to another type of specialist provision such as a school for autism or moderate learning difficulties (MLD), or transfer to Kilgarth or another SEMH school.

**What role do you play in supporting other schools?**
Kilgarth School is a Strategic Partner within the Weatherhead Teaching School Alliance and we have a history of supporting other schools. We provide CPD for other schools, including Behaviour Modification, Safeguarding, Restriction and Restraint. I enjoy collaborating with other schools to support the professional learning of colleagues. Apart from the Teaching School Alliance, we have many other contacts, including one with a prison, where the inmates were really keen to do something productive. So they've made furniture for our schools, shared their own mental health training with us and have re-conditioned mountain bikes for pupils at both schools to use.

**You are known for running a school without punishments. In an SEMH school, how does this work?**

Before I was a teacher, I was a forensic anthropologist and came to know some of the worst aspects of humanity, including through the Srebrenica genocide. This started me thinking that there must be a better way. I was very taken with Nelson Mandela's saying that 'No-one is born to hate', and his talk of being compassionate. So I've tried to replace punishments with compassion and to concentrate on relationships between the staff, between pupils, and between staff and pupils and it seems to work. We use Coaching, too, as a leadership style in order to help self-regulation and manage their responses to stress. We don't forget how a child behaves and we don't condone poor behaviour, but we always try to forgive.

**Do you use Proactive Classroom Management, which looks at the amount of opportunity students have to learn and the amount of time they are actively engaged in learning?**

For a start, I don't like the term 'behaviour management'. I'm a tough guy and I don't have a problem managing behaviour. What I want is to change or modify behaviour, which goes back to BF Skinner's idea of positive reinforcement. So, every day, we mark the pupils for effort and for behaviour. We notice when they do well and we praise them for it, however small the step. We send postcards home to underline the fact. When parents first receive one of these postcards, they often remark that it's the first time something positive has been said about their child instead of having to think, 'What's he done now?'

A rewards system needs to be based on what motivates the individual, what sort of reward they respond to and how they like it to be given. Extrinsic motivation can be worthwhile in itself as well as the possibility of leading to being intrinsically motivated.

**What would you like to do in the future, Steven?**

I've just co-authored a book with a colleague, Mick Simpson, about a school without sanctions. With my background as a forensic anthropologist and now an interest in neuroscience, I'd like to be in a position to influence the way we transform the educational outcomes of those who start with a disadvantage due to deprivation or other challenges.

## Conclusions

Both Steven Baker and Geri Cameron (whose school was mentioned earlier in the chapter, and will be mentioned again in Chapter 4), talk about the importance of giving these pupils, who have not engaged with education at previous schools, a second chance to make a success of their education and to stop, as Geri puts it, *the children's adversity outweighing their resilience.*

Although everyone agrees with early intervention, there is sometimes a reluctance to address pupils' needs as soon as they are identified rather than hoping that, given time, the difficulty will be resolved. For most pupils this will mean trying to give them the right kind of support for their mental health and emotional wellbeing in their current provision. However, for a small percentage, it may mean that a different environment will be needed. This in no way signifies failure on the part of the school or a failure on the part of the pupil, but it may not be reasonable to expect every school to cater for every child who comes their way, or, indeed, for every pupil to be able to flourish in the setting where they are placed. Where a move is indicated, it should be seen as a positive step, not as sending them off to a 'last resort' option.

It may be that a further impetus to recognising the importance of emotional wellbeing will be one of the long-term effects of the coronavirus and that, not only will it have made everyone more aware of mental health issues and the importance of addressing them before they become more entrenched, but it may have created an opportunity to rethink the ways schools work. Emotions and learning cannot be divorced from each other as they are inextricably linked. The next chapter looks at the strides that are being made to ensure that the Green Paper on Mental Health and other initiatives mean that educational establishments are better equipped to support the very wide range of emotional needs which are likely to be found in today's classrooms.

# References

Carpenter, B., and Egerton, J. (2016) *Girls and Autism: Flying under the Radar*. Tamworth: NASEN Publications.

Carpenter, B., Egerton, J., and Happe, F. (Editors) (2019) *Girls and Autism*. London: Routledge.

Children's Commissioner for England (2020) *Childhood in the Time of Covid*. Available from www.childrenscommissioner.gov.uk/wp-content/uploads/2020/09/cco-childhood-in-the-time-of-covid.pdf

The Children's Society (2019) *The Good Childhood Report 2019*. Available from www.childrenssociety.org.uk/sites/default/files/the_good_childhood_report_2019.pdf

The Children's Society (2020) *Life on Hold: Children's Well-Being and Covid*. Available from www.childrenssociety.org.uk/sites/default/files/2020-10/life-on-hold-childrens-well-being-and-covid-19.pdf

Colley, D., and Cooper, P. (Editors) (2017) *Attachment and Emotional Development in the Classroom: Theory and Practice*. London: Jessica Kingsley Publishers.

DfE (2014) *Behaviour and Discipline in Schools*. Available from https://assets.publishing.service.gov.uk/government/uploads/system/uploads/attachment_data/file/488034/Behaviour_and_Discipline_in_Schools_-_A_guide_for_headteachers_and_School_Staff.pdf

DfE (2015) *The SEND Code of Practice: 0–25 Years*. Available from www.gov.uk/government/publications/send-code-of-practice-0-to-25

DfE (2016 and 2018) *Mental Health and Behaviour in Schools: Departmental Advice for School Staff*. Available from https://assets.publishing.service.gov.uk/government/uploads/system/uploads/attachment_data/file/755135/Mental_health_and_behaviour_in_schools__.pdf

DoH and DfE (2017) *Transforming Children and Young People's Mental Health Provision: A Green Paper*. Available from https://assets.publishing.service.gov.uk/government/

uploads/system/uploads/attachment_data/file/664855/Transforming_children_and_young_people_s_mental_health_provision.pdf

H.M. Government (1999) *Saving Lives: Our Healthier Nation*. Available from https://assets.publishing.service.gov.uk/government/uploads/system/uploads/attachment_data/file/265576/4386.pdf

https://new.boxallprofile.org/

New Economics Foundation (NEF) (2011) *Five Ways to Wellbeing: New Applications, New Ways of Thinking*. Available from https://neweconomics.org/uploads/files/d80eba95560c09605d_uzm6b1n6a.pdf

NHS (2008) *5 Steps to Mental Well Being*. London: NHS (updated in 2020). Available from www.nhs.uk/conditions/stress-anxiety-depression/improve-mental-wellbeing/

Satchwell-Hirst, M. (2017) *Attachment and Emotional Development in the Classroom: Theory and Practice*. London: Jessica Kingsley Publishers.

Tes (2020) *FE Survey: Report in Tes January 23rd 2020*. London: Tes Global.

World Health Organisation (2014) *Towards a New Definition of Mental Health*. Available from www.ncbi.nlm.nih.gov/pmc/articles/PMC4471980/

www.mentallyhealthyschools.org.uk/resources/the-strengths-and-difficulties-questionnaire-sdq/

www.mind.org.uk/

# Chapter 2

# A pathway to progress

As mentioned in the previous chapter, there has been a gradual realisation of the importance of emotional wellbeing in young people as well as in adults. Some of the key milestones that demonstrate this come from both the health service and from education. This chapter considers how this increased awareness that young learners have had a raw deal has led to a concerted effort to do something about it. As so often happens, the momentum builds up through a succession of events until a consensus is reached about what needs to happen, how it will happen and who is responsible for bringing some coherence to the way forward.

It would take too long, and not be particularly helpful, to list everything that has happened since the turn of the century. However, it may be useful to trace the key events that led up to Future in Mind in 2015 (DoH and NHS, 2015) and, subsequently, to the Green Paper 'Transforming children and young people's mental health provision' in 2017 (DoH and DfE, 2017). One of the encouraging aspects that is apparent in considering the trail that has led to this point is the way that those involved have been prepared to leave their comfort zone and join together to enable improvements to take place. This can be seen from the way government departments have come out of their silos, people from different professional backgrounds have recognised each other's expertise, and mental health charities have grouped together to drive the agenda forward. There has been a general willingness to accept that, by working together, so much more can be achieved in giving mental health parity of esteem with physical health.

## The first steps to change

In 2011, the Coalition Government published a document called, 'No health without mental health' (H.M. Government, 2011). The strategy identified two overarching goals:

1  To improve the mental health and wellbeing of the population and keep people well

2    To improve outcomes for people with mental health problems through high quality services that are equally accessible to all

The following year, the Health and Social Care Act was passed and led to a reorganisation of services as set out below:

---

### Information point    Health and social care

The National Health Service (NHS) is the umbrella term for the publicly-funded healthcare systems of the United Kingdom (UK).

The Health and Social Care Act of 2012 (H.M. Government, 2012) led to Clinical Commissioning Groups (CCGs) being established to commission healthcare services for their local communities. They replaced the Primary Care Trusts (PCTs) run by groups of General Practitioners (GPs), but GPs are still members of CCGs.

Health and Wellbeing Boards (HWBs) bring together key players from across the services. They have a statutory duty to work with CCGs to produce a health and wellbeing strategy for their local population.

Public Health England (PHE) existed to improve the nation's health and wellbeing. It is due to be replaced by a National Institute for Health Protection (NIHP) by spring of 2021.

The National Institute for Health and Care Excellence (NICE) decides which drugs and treatments are available at the NHS in England. In other parts of the UK it is: the All Wales Medicines Strategy Group (AWMSG), the Northern Ireland (NI) Formulary and the Scottish Medicines Consortium in Scotland.

The Care Quality Commission (CQC) is the regulator for health and social care services in England. It has become well known in educational circles for its work with Ofsted on local area SEND inspections.

---

Although constant reorganisations can be unhelpful and slow down progress, the Health and Social Care Act is an example of encouraging joint collaboration, not just between health and social care, but through setting up an overarching organisation like the Health and Wellbeing Boards. A report in 2019 by the Local Government Association (LGA, 2019) concluded that HWBs were making a positive contribution to the future health and care outcomes identified in the NHS Long Term Plan (NHS, 2019), by putting prevention at the heart of what they do, rather than managing ill health better. Similarly, in 2018, the Department of Health (DoH) became the Department of Health and Social Care (DHSC), which was seen as a positive move in joining the services together.

## Children and Young People's Mental Health Taskforce (CYPMHT)

In 2012, a Children and Young People's Mental Health Taskforce (CYPMHT) was established. The lasting impact of its work was due, in no small part, to the wide range of people from across services, charities and other organisations, local authorities (LAs), schools, universities and many others, who were part of this taskforce.

### Future in Mind

Three years later, and in the same year as the SEND Code of Practice appeared – as mentioned in the opening chapter in relation to the change from BESD to SEMH – the DoH and NHS England published the results of the taskforce's work under the title: 'Future in Mind – promoting, protecting and improving children and young people's mental health and wellbeing'. The main themes are:

* Promoting resilience, prevention and early intervention
* Improving access to effective support – a system without tiers
* Care for the most vulnerable
* Accountability and transparency
* Developing the workforce
* Making change happen

At the time this document was published, two other documents appeared to complement it. The first of these was DfE's advice on counselling in schools (DfE, 2015) and the second was DfE-funded materials produced by the PSHE Association (2015) (supporting personal, social, health and economic (PSHE) education), which included resources for teaching about mental health and emotional wellbeing. (There is more about how these materials have been updated to fit in with the new relationships, sex and health education [RSHE] curriculum in Chapter 5).

The publication of Future in Mind helped to turn the tide in establishing a national system. In his foreword, Norman Lamb, at that time the Minister of State for Care and Support, talks about setting up the CYPMHT:

> We have funded the development of MindEd – giving more advice to health professionals about how to help young people with mental ill-health. We have put more mental health beds for young people in the

system. . . . But this isn't enough – we need to be ambitious if we want
children and young people to live happy, healthy lives. . . . Crucially, we
must make it much easier for a child or young person to seek help and
support in non-stigmatised settings.

(DoH and NHS, 2015: 3)

His use of the phrase 'non-stigmatised' is very telling, as it makes it clear that
one of the problems with young people being prepared to discuss their mental wellbeing as openly as their physical health has been the danger of being
stigmatised.

One of the many outcomes of Future in Mind, and in keeping with the
drive to move forward services for young people's wellbeing, NHS England
brought in Local Transformation Plans for each area of the country and, at the
same time, gave a push to the wider use of a programme from Children and
Adolescent Mental Health Services (CAMHS), to encourage the use of short-
term solutions for some of the less entrenched mental health difficulties young
people may have.

---

**Information point   Local Transformation Plans**

Local Transformation Plans for Children and Young People's Mental
Health and Wellbeing came about as a direct result of Future in Mind
and – as a result of all those involved in delivering services working
together – followed its aim of improving services and access to them.

The first of these Local Transformation Plans was published in 2015,
covering the whole of England. They are meant to be updated annually.
HWBs are involved in signing them off and they are published on the
websites of the CCGs.

The Plans also identify if local services are involved in the 'Children
and Young People's Improving Access to Psychological Therapies' service
transformation programmes (CYP IAPT), which offer short-term psychological therapies – mainly for conditions such as anxiety, depression
or stress – to young people up to the age of 19. Psychological therapies
are also referred to as 'talking therapies'. They have become increasingly
popular for helping those who have mild to moderate mental health
difficulties. They provide an opportunity for people to understand why
they feel as they do, work through those feelings and develop strategies
for moving forward.

---

Another outcome of Future in Mind is given in the case study that follows,
which demonstrates how, by working in partnership, a whole area has been

able to replicate the principles set out in the document to take forward the work on emotional health and wellbeing. This shows what can be achieved when the twin pillars of working and training come together.

### Case study of Future in Mind – Telford & Wrekin

In 2014, The Bridge School, which is a special school, and Newport Infant School – both designated teaching schools – were encouraged to form the Severn Teaching School Alliance in Telford, which offers initial teacher training (ITT) in conjunction with the University of Chester, as well as other professional qualifications. The Alliance is supported by over 60 primary, special and secondary schools which are strategic partners. The Alliance has its own team of School Improvement Specialists, Specialist Leaders of Education (SLEs) and National Leaders of Education (NLEs).

---

## Case study   Future in Mind – Telford & Wrekin

Future in Mind – Telford & Wrekin was established in November 2016 by the Severn Teaching School Alliance, in partnership with Public Health, Telford & Wrekin Council and Telford & Wrekin CCG to ensure that emotional health and wellbeing were high on the agenda of all the schools involved. These partners include all types of schools, as well as the Virtual School; the 0–25 Wellbeing Service; Strengthening Families; Health Visitors; School Nurses; and the private and voluntary sector. Each organisation nominates an Emotional Health and Wellbeing Lead (the most appropriate person within their setting). A service level agreement (SLA) provides:

- Termly professional development sessions linked to an identified emotional health and wellbeing need that Leads attend and then deliver continuous professional development (CPD) to their own staff and share good practice
- Each organisation has the slides to provide the training to their colleagues, plus any appropriate resources that will support the setting in providing an intervention to support mental health.

Some of the aspects of emotional health and wellbeing that have been covered so far are:

- Understanding mental health and wellbeing
- Developing assessment for wellbeing

- Understanding attachment and trauma
- Supporting young learners with autism, ADHD, stress, depression or anxiety
- Sleep
- The impact on Lesbian, Gay, Bisexual and Transgender (LGBT) children and young people's mental health
- Healthy relationships
- Emotion coaching
- The impact of technology on wellbeing
- Bereavement and loss
- Understanding self-harm
- Mindfulness

There are also regular updates from BEE-U and partners, including BEAM (an emotional and wellbeing drop-in centre for young people under 25 run by The Children's Society) and Kooth (online support services for children age 10+). Since its inception, the main emphasis of the project has been: prevention, early identification, and early help and support.

In the conversation that follows, Sian Deane, who has managed the Future in Mind – Telford & Wrekin project from the start, mentions her involvement with The Pilot Link Project, how her work runs alongside that of the Mental Health Trailblazers, and the work of CAMHS.

*In conversation with Sian Deane, project manager*

**Q.  What was your role in the development of Future in Mind – Telford & Wrekin?**

A.  When I was a local head teacher, and before the Mental Health Green Paper, Public Health Telford asked the Severn Teaching School Alliance to advise on how a sum of money it had acquired through commissioning might be used to support schools. So I submitted a Transformation Plan to show how the key concepts in Future in Mind could be rolled out. As the money only covered the first year, I showed how an SLA with schools could make it sustainable. Currently, there are 80 partners and the number is still growing. Although they are no longer involved financially, I report back each year to Public Health Telford, who continue to play a key role in supporting the project so they are kept abreast of its impact. In addition, I report back to the Severn Teaching School Alliance Board on a termly basis.

**Q. Where does the Link Programme fit in?**

A. Public Health Shropshire, which is the county that includes the unitary authority of Telford & Wrekin, was already engaged in the pilot phase of the Link Programme, so we made contact with the Anna Freud Centre which runs it and became part of the pilot. The programme is very helpful for areas that are still grappling with how everyone fits together and building relationships with them, much of which we'd been able to do through our Future in Mind project.

**Q. You have been able to have an emotional health and wellbeing lead in almost every one of your schools. Could you say a little more about the training they receive from you?**

A. At the beginning of each academic year, we put together three days of CPD, which includes access to the PowerPoint slides and the provision of recommended resources. Although every school has someone who is leading on mental health, they may decide to send a different member of staff depending on the topic under discussion. As I result, we have had members of the Senior Leadership Team (SLT), PSHE Leads, SENCOs, Pastoral Leads and Learning Mentors. As some schools are keen to send two members of staff, and we've managed to keep the SLA cost low, they have purchased two SLAs. Obviously, mental health is part of every teacher's role, but we've made sure every school has a named mental health lead and that person has designated time to carry out the role.

**Q. Do you know of other places running Future in Mind projects?**

A. I've worked with Worcestershire, Shropshire and Cheshire West which are all nearby, but also with Essex where I have a connection. Another grouping seems to be Barnsley, Bradford, Wakefield and Warrington, but I haven't had contact with them.

**Q. Have you made any changes to how the project operates in the light of the Mental Health Green Paper and the rollout of the Trailblazer Programme?**

A. As I was asked to be part of the bid writing for Telford & Wrekin to become a Mental Health Trailblazer in the second wave, I based the partnership aspect totally on what we were already doing with Future in Mind. It helped that I could show how successful we'd been over the four years of its existence. Now that the Mental Health Support Teams (MHSTs) are in place, I keep in touch with the Team Leader in our area so we are aware of each other's work.

In addition, BEE-U, BEAM and the MHST managers are members of the Health and Wellbeing Board's Panel which, since November 2019, has been meeting for schools to refer pupils to us. The Panel also includes the LA's EP Team; the Behaviour Support Team; CAMHS, Children's Social Care, the MHST managers, the social, emotional & mental health lead for the virtual school team; and BEAM, which is one of a number of services run by The Children's Society and is an emotional and wellbeing drop-in centre for young people under 25.

This means that schools no longer refer directly to CAMHS unless something is really urgent, so it helps to support all pupils with advice from professionals, those who really need to be seen by CAMHS and others who can be supported at a lower level of need.

**Q.  How do you see the future in terms of providing for young learners' mental health needs?**

A.  The Future in Mind project is based on the England Transformation Plan, NHS England, Future in Mind and the Government Green Paper for Mental Health. It has been successful because of this firm foundation and true inter-agency working, upskilling the school and partner workforce to identify, support and improve the mental health of children, their families and staff on a daily basis.

Feedback from colleagues illustrates that they have a good understanding of a variety of mental health conditions, how these may present themselves, and the strategies that can be used with non-clinical professionals. They have increased confidence when talking to parents and supporting children and young people. Group supervision is about to be introduced to support the work of the mental health leads and to strengthen the peer-to-peer support that has made the programme successful by breaking down barriers between professionals from different sectors – true inter-agency working.

Tina Rae, who has spent some time with us over the last four years, says she sees it as a model which is truly sustainable.

There needs to be a national programme but with flexibility for local autonomy and the ability to involve families and children. There needs to be inbuilt sustainability within this national programme so that it can continue without those involved having to worry about how long it will last but can go from strength to strength.

Expanding on Sian's wide-ranging discussion, CAMHS will be discussed shortly. Towards the end of the chapter, examples of two Mental Health Trailblazer areas are given. The Link Programme is covered in the next section.

## Training

The Link Programme is another direct outcome of Future in Mind and includes the idea of having a single point of contact between schools and mental health services. This programme and Mental Health First Aid (MHFA) training were in place before the Trailblazers appeared.

### The Link Programme

The 'Mental Health Services, Schools and Colleges Link Programme', known as 'The Link Programme' (Anna Freud Centre and DfE, 2020) is funded by the DfE, supported by NHS England and led by the Anna Freud National Centre for Children and Families. It began as a pilot which ran from Sept 2015 to May 2016, with the aim of bringing education and mental health practitioners together so that more young people would get the help and support they needed. The pilot was implemented by local CCGs, often with the support and active involvement of LAs.

An evaluation (DfE and NHS England, 2017) showed the pilot had resulted in significant improvements but the scheme would benefit from further testing. As a result, a second phase was launched which included sixth forms and vocational colleges for the first time. Following this second phase delivered to a much wider spread of educational settings, the DfE commissioned a partnership of twelve organisations, led by the Anna Freud Centre, to roll out the Link Programme over four years beginning in September 2019 to all schools and colleges in England. The twelve organisations include: CORC (Child Outcomes Research Consortium), Mind, MindEd, and Place2Be.

---

### Information point   The Link Programme

CCGs identify who should attend, including:

- The CCG Commissioning Lead
- A senior manager and practitioners from NHS England's Children and Young People's Mental Health Services (CYPMHS)
- A mental health lead from each school or college
- A member of the school or college SLT

Other professionals who can add to the richness of the workshops include:

- LA representatives and Educational Psychology Teams
- The voluntary community sector
- School governors
- Public Health Teams and GPs
- School and college nursing and counsellors
- Behaviour Support Teams
- Adoption Teams
- Safeguarding Teams
- Youth Offending Teams (YOTs)

---

The Link Programme is for people working in education and mental health services who have a role in improving mental health support in schools and colleges. The programme centres round two full-day workshops which are not consecutive. Around 20 schools and colleges attend at any one time, with schools being encouraged to send two members of staff if feasible. Rather than delay the programme, in the Autumn of 2020 the training was delivered online. There is further information about the Link Programme in a 2019–2020 Guide for CCGs.

### Other mental health courses

When she was Prime Minister, Theresa May made a commitment to provide mental health training for at least one member of staff in every secondary school in England. MHFA England, a company involved in providing training in this area for those working with adults, was given funding by the DHSC to run the first two years of a three-year youth MHFA in schools programme. This was a one-day course which aimed to train around 1,000 secondary staff per year. For the third year of the programme, the training was offered by the Anna Freud Centre, under the title of Mental Health Awareness Training (MHAT). This training was put on hold due to COVID-19.

However, a growing number of courses of varying lengths have become available, both from individual providers and from national organisations, including MHFA, the Anna Freud Centre, Place2Be, the St John Ambulance, the Healthy London Partnership, and Nasen – National Association for Special Education Needs. Lorraine Petersen, who was, for many years, CEO of Nasen – a charitable membership organisation supporting all education practitioners – explains how she was keen to become involved with children and young people's mental health and wellbeing. From January 2021, Nasen changed its tiered model of membership charges to no charge for all individuals working in educational settings across the UK. There remains a small charge for international colleagues.

### In conversation with Lorraine Petersen, former CEO of Nasen

**Q. What made you decide to add mental health training to your SEND expertise?**

A. When the current SEND Code of Practice came out in 2015 and I saw the terminology had changed from BESD to SEMH, I realised that, as well as an overlap between mental health and SEND, there were wider implications. I'd always been interested in the impact of social and emotional difficulties on children's behaviour, so decided this was the right time to find out more about mental health issues.

**Q. How do you see the overlap between SEMH being part of the SENCO's strategic role and the MH part also coming under the senior mental health lead (SMHL)?**

A. The only definitive description we've had so far about the role of the strategic lead for mental health is a brief description in the Green Paper. To start with, many SENCOs told me it had been assumed that they would take on the role, but I saw it as a massive job. To me, there are three key posts that need to work together: the SENCO, the designated safeguarding lead (DSL) and the SMHL. Whereas there is mandatory training to be a SENCO and they must be a qualified teacher, nothing has been said about who can take on the role of SMHL or how it fits in, for instance, with a pastoral lead.

**Q. What is the difference between Mental Health First Aid (MHFA) and Youth Mental Health First Aid?**

A. MHFA is a Community Interest Company and its courses were mainly for big businesses, etc. Having won the contract for every secondary school to receive training for one person, the company launched YMHFA, with courses aimed at those supporting young people between the ages of 8 and 16 years. Personally, I think they should include younger children. In 2019, the contract went to the Anna Freud Centre who started doing Mental Health Awareness Training (MHAT) instead. However, MHFA still delivers a number of courses: a half-day course for awareness raising, a one-day course to become a MH Champion and a two-day course for MH First Aiders.

**Q. What is your role as a qualified Mental Health First Aid Instructor and the training this enables you to deliver.**

A. The two-day course gives a good overview of the different types of mental health issues young people may suffer from. It includes information about suicide which is tough to deliver and tough for people to hear. MHFA is the sole provider of the course to become an instructor. Having been trained, I prefer to organise my own training, but some trainers prefer to have MHFA make all the arrangements for them. In either case, the trainer must use the materials provided by MHFA, which include: a comprehensive manual, a folder and a useful collection of PowerPoint slides which are updated.

**Q. When the National Youth MHFA in schools programme was being run by MHFA England, it said it qualified participants to become Mental Health Champions, but they now have a separate course to become a Champion.**

A. Yes, that is the situation. As well as the YMHFA one-day course to become a Mental Health Champion, Place2Be also run a Mental Health Champions Training, which has three levels of training: a foundation course, a course for teachers and a longer programme for school leaders.

**Q. Do you know if the training to become a Wellbeing Ambassador is for young people rather than adults?**

A. A Wellbeing Ambassador is often a pupil with responsibility for helping to promote the wellbeing of other pupils. Sometimes, there may be several wellbeing ambassadors in a school, each with a particular focus such as anti-bullying, mental health, online safety, etc. At one school I've worked with, for example, which is Baxter College, part of the Severn Academies Educational Trust (two secondary schools and five primary schools), they have many staff trained in MHFA as well as several student Wellbeing Ambassadors.

Q. **What is your one-day training course on the Wellbeing Toolkit for mental health leads in schools (MHLS) and your Train the Trainer programme?**

A. As well as delivering YMHFA courses, I also run shorter courses, including one aimed at teachers taking on the mental health lead role. I've linked this course to Tina Rae's Wellbeing Toolkit for mental health leads (MHLs). Then I realised that because the Toolkit is such an extensive resource, I might need to offer a Train the Trainer course linked to this resource so that those who had been trained could help their staff in finding their way through the materials and knowing what's there. So I started a Train the Trainer course specifically for this. I've had many Pastoral Leads and School Leaders accessing the course, more than teachers who say they are the mental health lead.

Q. **Do you know of other general courses to do with mental health and emotional wellbeing that ought to be mentioned?**

A. The main players I've come across in the field of mental health training, in addition to the ones already mentioned, are: Natasha Devon, a former government mental health champion; Dr Pooky Knightsmith, who describes herself as an autistic mum of two, who has had her own battles with PTSD, anorexia, self-harm and depression; and REAL Training, which was founded in 2004 by three educational psychologists and runs courses at all levels. There's also Barnardos and the NSPCC.

Q. **Is there anything else you'd like to mention, whether or not it's about training?**

A. I've been very impressed by the PSHE Association's mental health lesson plans, which cover nursery to sixth form. They have free resources as well as extra ones you have access to by becoming a member.

    YoungMinds has 'Our Parents Helpline' which is available in England, Scotland, Wales and Northern Ireland.

In addition to the courses Lorraine mentions, other sources of training are part of the rollout of the Green Paper.

## Green Paper on Mental Health

As mentioned at the start of this chapter, the Green Paper on Mental Health built on the work of the Children and Young People's Mental Health Coalition (CYPMHC) and Future in Mind. This had three key elements. In brief these are:

1  Every school and college to identify a *designated senior lead for mental health*
2  *Mental Health Support Teams* (MHSTs), supervised by NHS staff, to provide extra capacity to schools and colleges in terms of early intervention and ongoing help

3 A *four-week waiting* time for access to specialist NHS children and young people's mental health services to be trialled

A year later, the government followed this up with a further document giving details of the response to the consultation that had taken place and setting out what the 'next steps' would be in order to implement the proposals.

## Designated senior lead for mental health

The title of this role was changed to 'senior mental health lead' (SMHL) in order to differentiate the role more clearly from the existing DSL. The government said this role would not be mandatory but that schools would be 'incentivised' to appoint such a person, who would be able to take a strategic overview of pupils' emotional wellbeing, in a similar way to a SENCO having the strategic oversight of pupils with SEND. The training was due to be rolled out from September 2019 onwards, but the timetable was delayed by the pandemic.

## Mental Health Support Teams (MHSTs)

The government said it would test out how these teams would work through having a number of Trailblazer areas, with the first ones operational by the end of 2019. MHSTs are made up of groups of around four education mental health practitioners (EMHPs) together with their supervisors and administrative support. MHSTs will carry out three roles:

- To deliver evidence-based interventions to young learners with mild to moderate mental health needs
- To support the SMHL to develop a whole-school or college approach
- To liaise with external specialist providers in the area in order to help young people to access the right support and stay in education

MHSTs are due to cover a quarter of the country by 2022/23. They are a key part of helping to manage young learners within schools and colleges who have mental health issues so that they can be addressed earlier and fewer will need to overburden the services run by CAMHS. However, the teams will also be providing a link to more specialised services when they are needed. Many will be based in educational settings.

## A four-week waiting time

Some of the Trailblazer areas were also asked to pilot ways of reducing waiting times for children and young people with more significant mental health needs so that they would have a maximum of a four-week wait to access more specialised provisions.

### Education mental health practitioners (EMHPs)

While not specifically mentioned in the three points listed previously, EMHPs are at the heart of the MHSTs. They are based in MHSTs and supervised by NHS staff, while their role is to work in educational settings. Their training is university-based, lasts for a year and results in a postgraduate diploma. The first cohort began their training in September 2018, with further intakes in January and September each year. The course consists of academic and supervised practice learning across mental health services and educational settings, including primary and secondary schools, and FE colleges.

The universities currently training EMHPs are:

- Edge Hill University
- Greater Manchester Mental Health Psychological Therapies Training Centre
- King's College, London
- University College London (UCL)
- University of Derby
- University of East Anglia
- University of Exeter
- University of Northampton
- University of Northumbria
- University of Reading
- University of Sheffield
- University of Sussex

The programme is a shared initiative between the DfE and the DHSC and supports the government's priority to increase access to mental health and wellbeing support for children and young people in schools and colleges.

One point of proof that mental health and emotional wellbeing are on an upward trajectory is that changes in government and a new prime minister have made no difference to the path of progress. Furthermore, there will at last be a continuum of provision from support in the classroom to specialist services:

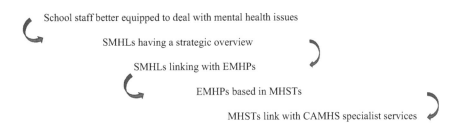

School staff better equipped to deal with mental health issues

SMHLs having a strategic overview

SMHLs linking with EMHPs

EMHPs based in MHSTs

MHSTs link with CAMHS specialist services

How these newer roles fit in with existing posts and provision is the topic of the next chapter.

# Child and Adolescent Mental Health Services (CAMHS)

It may be worth mentioning at this point that CAMHS is not a single entity but covers all NHS services which assess and treat young people with emotional, behavioural or mental health difficulties. These services are provided by a range of organisations including: NHS mental health and community trusts, LAs, and the private and voluntary sectors. CAMHS may be located in places such as hospitals, Child and Family Clinics and GP surgeries. Most CAMHS services work with the whole family to support a young person's health. This might include the family coming along to assessment and treatment appointments together, depending on the child's age and what level of involvement they want. Teenagers have to move from CAMHS to adult mental health services (AMHS) when they reach a certain age, often at 18 years, but this can vary in different areas.

---

**Information point   Child and Adolescent Mental Health Services (CAMHS)**

Child and Adolescent Mental Health Services are NHS-provided services in England and Wales that assess and treat young people, generally until school-leaving age, who are having emotional, behavioural or mental health difficulties.

There are local NHS CAMHS services around the UK, with teams made up of nurses, therapists, psychologists, support workers and social workers, as well as other professionals.

Increasingly, the term CYPMHS is being used instead of CAMHS. In addition, some areas have taken to using other terms such as 'Healthy Young-Minds', 'Emotional Wellbeing and Mental Health Service' (EWMHS), or, as in the previous case study about Future in Mind – Telford & Wrekin, 'Bee U' is the emotional health and wellbeing service for people living in Shropshire.

Another change is a shift from talking about four tiers of support to moving to the 'Thrive Framework' of five needs-based groupings.

(Association for Child and Adolescent Mental Health [ACAMH] is an association for everyone who works in CAMHS settings and has existed for over 60 years. It runs conferences, training events, special interest groups and master classes, in addition to publishing journals.)

---

For some time, CAMHS services have been described as having four tiers or levels:

- Tier 1   Universal services provided by health visitors, school nurses, GPs, teachers
- Tier 2   Targeted services where some specialist input is required

- Tier 3    Specialist support from CAMHS
- Tier 4    Specialist support from CAMHS including in-patient care

Under this description, EMHPs will be able to support schools in providing Tier 1 and 2 support, as well as being the route to more specialised care when it is needed. It has sometimes been argued that the four-tier model is unhelpful and reinforces distinctions between different types of services when an integrated service structured around the needs of children and young people would be more effective. This was picked up in the Future in Mind publication, in a chapter headed: 'A system without tears'.

Seeking a more flexible system, the 'Thrive Framework' is a conceptual model for ensuring needs-led service planning and review. It was developed by mental health professionals from the Anna Freud National Centre for Children and Families, and the Tavistock and Portman NHS Foundation Trust. The Framework is supported by training, resources and a community of practice.

The five categories of support, rather than the four tiers, are:

> Thriving
>> Getting advice and signposting
>>> Getting help
>>>> Getting more help
>>>>> Getting risk support

At the time of writing, both models exist. The other change that has come through is that an increasing number of CAMHS services are using different descriptions, including CYPMHS, as well as names which do not include the words 'mental health'.

## The Trailblazer Programme

The Green Paper led to the setting up of the Trailblazers. The first 25 Trailblazer areas were announced in December 2018. These included 12 areas that are also testing a four-week waiting time. A further 57 sites were confirmed in July 2019 and led to the development of 123 more MHSTs during 2020. To give an insight into how these developments are working out in practice, two Trailblazer areas are described. The first is in Hertfordshire, which was in the first wave of Trailblazers, and the second is about one of the London Trailblazer areas which began later.

### Hertfordshire

Hertfordshire covers a large geographical area. It has around 500 schools, four FE colleges and the University of Hertfordshire. There are two CCGs: East and

North Hertfordshire CCG and Herts Valleys CCG. Each MHST in the CCG areas are linked to around 20 schools and colleges.

Hertfordshire is one of ten 'iThrive accelerator sites', working towards embedding the Thrive principles and methodology across all emotional well-being and mental health services, including CAMHS.

*Case study of Maple Primary School*

One of the schools to be among the first to benefit from having an EMHP is Maple Primary School in St Albans.

## Case study Maple   Primary School, St Albans

The school has around 250 pupils aged 4 to 11. There is a unit for pupils who are hearing impaired (HI) and have been assessed as having the potential to develop speech and language without needing to sign. Heathlands School for profoundly deaf pupils, who are taught through Total Communication including British Sign Language (BSL) and Sign Supported English (SSE), is in the same city. This means that the whole continuum of hearing impairment is catered for.

Creating a happy school is the core aim of Maple School, where the physical and mental health of pupils and staff is seen as a prerequisite to learning. One of the ways of achieving this is by nurturing a sense of wellbeing and an awareness of the academic, physical, social, cultural, emotional and spiritual needs of others. PSHE is an integral part of the curriculum. A pupil-led Playground Squad organises various lunchtime activities to promote happy and safe playtimes, while school and class councils are another way of developing a sense of responsibility in the pupils.

Sex and drugs education are an important part of the PSHE Scheme of Work for Year 6 pupils, who are also made aware of their legal responsibilities through re-enacting a Magistrates Court. In this, they are assisted by the head teacher, Timothy Bowen, having been a former magistrate of many years standing.

The grounds are used to promote a variety of outdoor learning opportunities – for example, in science, geography and PE – as well as for extracurricular activities.

Outside, there is a large playing field, two playgrounds, a conservation/wildlife area, together with an outdoor learning/play area for the reception class.

Shanti Johnson, who is the Deputy Head and the Wellbeing Co-ordinator at the school, explains how having an EMHP has enhanced what the school is able to provide to support pupil and staff wellbeing.

IN CONVERSATION WITH SHANTI JOHNSON

**Q. Did you volunteer to be the link with the EMHP or how was the decision made? Are you known as the senior mental health lead (SMHL) or by another title in this role?**

A. I was asked by the head if I'd be interested and I jumped at the chance. As I was already known as the Wellbeing Co-ordinator, and this description, fits in with colleagues who are co-ordinators of subjects, we agreed to keep my current description.

**Q. How does your role fit in with the SENCO, in terms of SEMH being one of the four broad areas of need?**

A. The previous deputy head used to be the SENCO but has now retired. We now have a SENCO who is part-time and we work closely together.

**Q. Apart from class teachers, are there any other roles you link with in particular?**

A. I am part of the safeguarding team, which the head leads. We have a separate co-ordinator for PSHE, but as part of my role as overall curriculum co-ordinator, I've been asked to look at the new relationships education curriculum. In our school, Looked After Children come under the remit of the SENCO.

**Q. Have you or other staff received any training in this area, e.g., Mental Health First Aid, The Link Programme, SMHL training, or is there any training planned for the future?**

A. I have taken the mental health lead two-day training, which has enabled me to deliver level 1 training to the rest of the staff. This included all teaching staff and many teaching assistants as well.

**Q. How much time is the EMHP able to give the school? I realise this may have been interrupted by COVID-19 this year. Does it include pupils in the HI Unit if needed?**

A. Our EMHP, Carolyn, comes in for half a day every week. So far, it has been mainly to meet and support parents, for instance those struggling with anxiety issues, either in themselves or their child/ren. She delivers training sessions for them. A few who hoped the problem would simply be taken away from them benefitted less than those who attended all the sessions. They saw it as a partnership and have reaped the benefits.

**Q. What difference do you think having an EMHP has made to the pupils and staff?**

A. Early on, Carolyn talked about her role at a staff meeting, so everyone had met her and knew what her role was. They will now approach her to discuss any difficulties.

Earlier this year, we made a successful bid for £500 from the LA which helped towards the cost of holding a Wellbeing Week and the LA contributed towards the cost. Carolyn gave an assembly so all the pupils knew who she was and she followed this up by going into each class. She focused mainly on the importance of self-regulation and how you need to have strategies to help yourself when you're feeling anxious or low. The lessons were pitched at different levels depending on the age group she was addressing. We are thinking of having another Wellbeing Week again next year.

Carolyn has also given a Transition Workshop to Y6 pupils with her line manager. This year, it had to be online because of the virus. She has also given online support to parents this summer and is part of a central telephone support line specifically for parents to discuss their concerns about COVID-19.

We had planned to give each member of staff a 20 to 30 minute slot with Carolyn to talk about their own, or their pupils', wellbeing but that has been placed on hold due to the pandemic.

**Q. Are there any changes the school as a whole has made as a result of having an EMHP?**

A.  Having an EMHP has definitely increased the school's focus on wellbeing. There are more open discussions about mental health and it has become more the norm to talk about it. Although I don't consider myself to be an expert, it has always been an area of interest and I have read a great deal about it. I always make it a feature of my assemblies. I also think it's reassuring for parents to know that we have this link with the NHS. Both Carolyn and I see her role as being focused on prevention. The focus on parents – their anxieties and those of their children – is all part of this approach.

**Q. Have you met anyone else through being a Trailblazer school?**

A.  I went to one meeting at the beginning to find out what it would mean to be part of the Trailblazer Programme and I've met Carolyn's line manager. At one point, someone from the DfE came in. However, I know that she is the main link and will take forward queries to colleagues if there is a need.

**Q. Please feel free to add anything else you think might be relevant.**

A.  My main aim is to make everyone more aware, to know we all need to look after our mental health and to learn strategies to cope.

In the next chapter, which is about roles and responsibilities, there is a conversation with Carolyn McKay, who is the EMHP attached to Maple Primary School. She explains exactly what this newer role entails.

### London

The second example of a Trailblazer comes from London, where Central and West London CCGs and the charity 'Mind', worked with Westminster, and with Kensington & Chelsea LAs, to establish MHSTs from the end of 2019 onwards. Two of these MHSTs are in Westminster, where Kathryn Pugh is the head teacher of The St Marylebone CE School. Although this is a more recent Trailblazer than the one in Hertfordshire, Kathryn was able to give some useful insights into the effects of being in a Trailblazer area, and, at the same time, to comment more generally on other matters relating to the mental health and wellbeing of the staff and pupils in her school.

*In conversation with Kathryn Pugh, Head Teacher, The St Marylebone CE School*

**Q. Do you have a member of staff who leads on mental health and wellbeing? If so, are they called a senior mental health lead or do they have a different title?**

A. Yes. The member of staff is called the mental health lead. They are also a head of year, have a safeguarding role and are involved in the school's PSHE programmes. We have also appointed a second person in charge of mental health, who has a specific focus on the 6th Form.

**Q. How does the role of being responsible for mental health fit in with other roles in the school, such as the SENCO, the designated teacher for LAC, the DSL, and Pastoral Care staff?**

A. The school is committed to the involvement of all staff in support of the mental health and wellbeing of their students. Specifically, there is a very strong team approach called *RAS – Referral and Assessment Team*, which meets regularly. It consists of the mental health lead, the director of SEN, relevant heads of year, and safeguarding staff. They plan appropriate support for students – within the school or from external providers.

**Q. Is the mental health lead involved with the development or delivery of the RSE and health curriculum?**

A. Yes. The mental health lead works with the PSHE Leads on this and it has been an essential part of the school's curriculum for some time.

**Q. Have staff had any mental health training, for instance through The Link Programme or Mental Health First Aid (MHFA)?**

A. The staff as a whole have not had any specific training, but the mental health lead has cascaded the training and information she's received to pastoral staff. The PSHE Lead, the second person in charge of Mental Health, the mentoring team and some other Heads of Year have also had various experiences of mental health training.

**Q. How did you become involved in the Westminster Trailblazer?**
Westminster became involved with the Trailblazer Programme in September 2019, as did the school. The ongoing development of the programme has been slowed down with the onset of COVID-19.

Q. **Is one of the Mental Health Support Teams (MHSTs) based in your school or have you met members of your nearest team?**
No, there isn't a team based in the school, but we have been allocated two Education Mental Health Practitioners (EMHPs) from the local MHST. Each one gives the school half a day a week, making a total of one day a week of support. The EMHPs are involved in the RAS meetings and subsequent interventions.

Q. **What difference do you think being part of the Trailblazer Programme will make to the school as a whole?**
The school has a very strong and ongoing commitment to supporting students' mental health needs. We value, appreciate and obtain all the additional support we can access in order to strengthen the provision we currently offer. The Trailblazer Programme has, and will, create opportunities for this to happen.

Q. **Do you think it is likely to result in any changes to the way the school meets the mental health and wellbeing needs of pupils, staff and families?**
The powerful ethos the school has to support everyone with their wellbeing and mental health will only be enhanced by having additional provision to existing services. The school strongly seeks to reduce the stigma of mental health. It supports its students in their management of 'normal' issues that arise with teenagers. We seek to empower our pupils and support the staff in recognising and responding to the additional issues that arise across the mental health spectrum, and subsequently provide the support that is needed.

## Conclusions

Although there have been criticisms of the time it will take to put everything in place as a result of the Green Paper and the work of the Trailblazers, at least the work is under way and will introduce a scale of collaboration between the health and education services which should go some way towards solving the problem of earlier intervention and support. This includes the urgent need to sort out young people's mental health issues before they become more entrenched and for school staff to be better trained to know how to identify those at risk and how to support them. Although the pandemic has added to what was already a lengthy timetable before the whole of England is included, at least the need for education and health to work together is embedded in what is envisaged.

After touching on some of the names who have influenced the approach to children and young people's emotional development, the next chapter concentrates on how the new roles that are appearing can complement those which already exist. Examples are given of how different educational settings have made the most of an opportunity to strengthen the support they offer already to improve the wellbeing of the whole school community.

## References

Anna Freud Centre and DfE (2020) *Mental Health Services and Schools and Colleges Link Programme 2019–2020: A Guide for CCG Leads.* Available from www.annafreud.org/ schools-and-colleges/research-and-practice/the-link-programme/ccg-leads/

DfE (2015) *Counselling in Schools: A Blueprint for the Future.* Available from www.gov.uk/ government/publications/counselling-in-schools

DfE, and NHS England (2017) *Mental Health Services and School Link Pilot: Evaluation.* Available from www.gov.uk/government/publications/mental-health-services-and-schools-link-pilot-evaluation

DoH, and DfE (2017) *Transforming Children and Young People's Mental Health Provision: A Green Paper.* Available from https://assets.publishing.service.gov.uk/government/ uploads/system/uploads/attachment_data/file/664855/Transforming_children_and_ young_people_s_mental_health_provision.pdf

DoH, and NHS (2015) *Future on Mind: Promoting, Protecting and Improving Our Children and Young People's Mental Health and Wellbeing.* Available from https://assets.publishing.service. gov.uk/government/uploads/system/uploads/attachment_data/file/414024/Childrens_ Mental_Health.pdf

H.M. Government (2011) *No Health without Mental Health: Cross Government Outcomes Strategy.* Available from www.gov.uk/government/publications/the-mental-health-strategy-for-england

H.M. Government (2012) *Health and Social Care Act.* Available from www.ncbi.nlm.nih. gov/pmc/articles/PMC4523576/

Local Government Association (LGA) (2019) *What a Difference a Place Makes: The Growing Impact of Health and Wellbeing Boards.* Available from https://local.gov.uk/ what-difference-place-makes-growing-impact-health-and-wellbeing-boards

NHS (2019) *The NHS Long Term Plan.* Available from www.england.nhs.uk/long-term-plan/

PSHE Association (2015) *A Curriculum for Life.* Available from www.pshe-association.org. uk/curriculum-and-resources/resources/curriculum-life-case-statutory-pshe-education

# Chapter 3

# Realigning roles and responsibilities

It is sometimes said that a theory only lasts until the next one comes along. Although there are times this is true, elements of previous theories often survive alongside newer thinking, at least until 'the theory of everything' exists as something other than a film about the physicist, Stephen Hawking. The first part of this chapter is about some of those who have influenced current thinking about how children mature, particularly in terms of their social and emotional development. Being aware of the usual pattern of development makes it easier to spot when a young person's behaviour gives cause for concern, or, as Colley D. and Cooper P. put it:

> Our role as professionals in schools is to understand that all behaviour is a form of communication of an unmet need. These children require us to set firm boundaries for them and to offer structures and routines. But they also require us to understand the gaps in their emotional learning and to provide opportunities for the "missed early experiences" associated with emotional competency to be revisited.
>
> (2017: 27)

## Linking theories to present-day practice

Many people have had a significant impact on our understanding of young learners who give cause for concern, referred to on the cover of O'Regan's book (2006), as those who *Can't Learn, Won't Learn, and Those Who Simply Don't Care Whether They Learn or Not*. While there is space to pick out only a few well-known names, it may be helpful to do so as a reminder of why they continue to arouse interest.

Piaget (1896–1980) saw children's development in terms of four stages of cognitive development:

- The sensorimotor stage
- The preoperational stage
- The concrete operational stage
- The formal operational stage

Although his work was criticised by both Vygotsky and Bruner for being too rigid, rather than seeing learning as a continuous process, Piaget's views on children needing to be active learners continue to be relevant. His thinking influenced the Plowden Report (Central Advisory Council for Education, 1967), which endorsed more group work and learning through play. Susan Isaacs (1885–1948) also emphasised the importance of play as a form of self-expression, enabling children to release their real feelings safely and to practise ways of dealing with a range of emotions. She helped facilitate the move away from the idea that children do not learn unless they are scolded or smacked.

B. F. Skinner (1904–1990) and others from the behaviourist branch of psychology also disagreed with Piaget, but this was because behaviourism is concerned with observable behaviour rather than with the thinking and emotions that may underlie that behaviour. Skinner saw Pavlov's notion of 'classical conditioning' as being too simplistic, preferring his own version of 'operant conditioning'. This views people's behaviour as being guided by the consequences of what will happen to them, so the behaviour can be reinforced by rewards or punishments, making it more or less likely that it will recur. This approach could be seen as compatible with DfE guidance:

> Schools should have in place a range of options and rewards to reinforce and praise good behaviour, and clear sanctions for those who do not comply with the school's behaviour policy.
>
> (2016: para 21)

It is a system to which the majority of pupils may respond, but, as was noted in the case study at the end of Chapter 1, there are pupils for whom other approaches will be needed.

Vygotsky (1896–1934) may be best known for what he called, 'the zone of optimal development'. This he described as the gap between what children could discover on their own and their level of potential development under adult guidance or in collaboration with more capable peers:

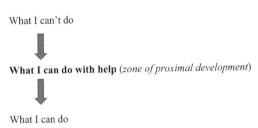

What I can't do

**What I can do with help** (*zone of proximal development*)

What I can do

Vygotsky used the term 'scaffolding' which is still in use today. This same approach may be thought of in terms of emotional development and the help a child may need in recognising their own and other people's emotions, and then learning how to control their responses.

Maslow (1908–1970) was one of the founders of humanistic psychology, which tries to help people fulfil their potential and maximise their wellbeing rather than concentrating on dysfunction. Maslow believed that both Freud's psychoanalytic theory and Skinner's behavioural theory were too focused on the negative aspects of existence and neglected the potential of human beings to be creative. He argued that some basic needs have to be met before a person is able to move forward. He described these as follows:

Self-actualisation
Esteem
Belongingness
Safety
Physiological

Although not universally accepted, Maslow's framework is mentioned here because of the link with the unmet needs that may lie behind mental health concerns. At a physiological level, a child who lacks food, water, shelter or sleep is not in a good place to learn. After their physiological needs have been met, children need to feel they are safe. If they live in fear and anxiety, particularly for prolonged periods, they are prone to developing mental health issues. If a child lacks a sense of social belonging, they are likely to lack confidence and self-esteem. Although it may not be within everyone's grasp to reach self-actualisation, particularly for those who have more fundamental unmet needs, Maslow (1943) felt it was important to have a goal to strive for.

Carl Rogers (1902–1987) also took a humanistic approach and agreed with Maslow's main assumptions. However, he added the idea that for a person to develop through the stages, they need the right environment. This means being listened to and being accepted, which he described as 'unconditional positive regard'. Rogers (1961) suggested that people who are able to self-actualise are more likely to have received unconditional positive regard from others, especially their parents, in childhood.

### Information point    Conditional and unconditional positive regard

*Conditional positive regard* is where positive regard, praise and approval depend upon the child behaving in ways their parents see as correct. Hence the child is not loved for the person he or she is, but only on the condition that he or she behaves in ways approved by the parent(s). A person who constantly seeks approval from other people may have experienced conditional positive regard as a child.

*Unconditional positive regard,* on the other hand, means accepting and respecting others as they are without judgment or evaluation. It means

> parents, significant others or a therapist accept the person for who he or she is, and their regard is not withdrawn if the person does something wrong or makes a mistake. The consequences of unconditional positive regard are that the person feels free to try things out and to make mistakes.

Although it may be rare for a person to reach self-actualisation, Rogers saw it, not as a destination but a journey: a process of becoming and changing on the way.

John Bowlby (1907–1990) was well known for making links between early experiences and later behaviours that may stem from disrupted and disturbed childhoods. This led to what became known as 'attachment theory', since then it has become a prominent part of trying to understand the behaviour of children and young people who struggle with their emotions. Bowlby helped us to understand why a child who feels unloved may believe they are unlovable and how attachment issues will stand in the way of their progress. It has also helped us to realise that treating everyone in the same way may not be the answer (Bowlby, 1944).

Daniel Goleman (1946–) in his double role of psychologist and journalist, brought his ideas on 'emotional intelligence' and 'social intelligence' into the public arena through his writing. Although his ideas have influenced the business world, his impact has been felt even more in education, where many now accept that emotional intelligence may be as important as intellectual prowess. In his book on emotional intelligence, Goleman talks about why teenagers are not skilled in settling disputes:

> One reason they are so poor at this basic life skill is that, as a society we have not bothered to make sure every child is taught the essentials of handling anger or resolving conflicts positively – nor have we bothered to teach empathy, impulse control, or any other of the fundamentals of emotional competency. . . . Shouldn't we be teaching these most essential skills for life to every child – now more than ever? And if not now, when?
> (1996: 286/7)

As well as understanding some of the reasons why young people behave as they do, the kind of support they might need and how they respond to different approaches, it may be useful at this point to reflect on the nature of emotions.

## Understanding emotions and behaviour

In essence, an emotion is a physiological response to a situation which causes us to act in a certain way. For instance, we may react to fear with an innate fight or flight response, which triggers the release of hormones preparing us to cope with the situation or to escape from it. Some children have difficulty recognising their own emotions, let alone those of other people, and therefore find it harder to regulate their impulses.

Although there is no universal agreement about how many main emotions there are, it is often accepted that there are six basic human emotions, all of which are visible through facial expression. According to Ekman these are hardwired into the brain to ensure survival. What may be less widely known is that these six are discernible in the first six months of life. They are:

- Fear
- Anger
- Happiness or joy
- Sadness
- Disgust
- Surprise

(Cole's *Nebraska Symposium*, 1971)

Many other common emotions can be listed, such as: anticipation, contempt, excitement, hate, jealousy, loneliness, love, trust, etc. Although the words 'emotions' and 'feelings' are sometimes used interchangeably, an emotion is an instinctive physical reaction to an event, while feeling is to do with how we respond to that emotional experience.

## Wellbeing and happiness

When in 2006 Anthony Seldon, at that time Master of Wellington College, abandoned GCSEs and introduced Happiness Lessons, many people were amazed that this should happen in one of the bastions of academic standards, a leading public school. Since then, Seldon has helped to found the charity, 'Action for Happiness', whose patron is Tenzin Gyatso, better known as His Holiness the Dalai Lama.

Along with a heightened interest in happiness and emotional wellbeing have come attempts to see how they might be measured. In a guide to measuring children's wellbeing produced by the NEF in conjunction with Action for Children, it suggested that:

> It is helpful to think of children's wellbeing as a dynamic process, in which a child's external circumstances (e.g., their socioeconomic background, family circumstances, physical surroundings) are constantly interacting with their individual characteristics (e.g., their personality, cognitive ability and so on) to satisfy . . . their needs and thus build psychological resources, capabilities and positive interactions with the world around them.

(2009: 2)

Roger Morgan, Children's Rights Director for England (a post that since 2014 has been absorbed by the work of the Children's Commissioner) carried out a project that resulted in 'The Children's Happiness Scale', which used statements children made about what made them happy or unhappy. Roger wrote about what emerged unexpectedly from analysing the results:

> So it looks as if we are actually measuring unhappiness, not happiness itself. Happiness seemed to be more 'not being unhappy' than as being something separate in itself. Children in our discussions indeed agreed over things that usually made a child unhappy – but told us that what makes you happy is very individual to you.
>
> (2014: 6)

This ties in with one of the definitions in the first chapter about wellbeing not being the same for everyone, and also with Maslow's idea that the self-actualisation we might aim for will be different for each one of us.

## Supporting social and emotional wellbeing

Moving on from how wellbeing and happiness might be measured, a project at University College London (UCL) Centre for Inclusive Education looked at how to help schools support pupils' social and emotional wellbeing. It has been named The SWERL Project, standing for 'Supporting Wellbeing, Emotional Resilience and Learning'. The project involves a team of three staff members from primary or secondary schools, Post-16, or alternative provision (AP), who are committed to supporting whole-school wellbeing. The team is a combination of a head teacher/member of the SLT; school mental health lead; SENCO/inclusion manager, governor, school counsellor; and an enthusiastic teacher or high level teaching assistant (HLTA).

SWERL is one of a series of Knowledge Exchange Programmes (KEPs) run by UCL, which are designed to emphasise a two-way exchange of learning between researchers and practitioners. In the conversation with Amelia Roberts that follows, she mentions using Kotter's Theory of Change (1996). This has eight stages to achieving the change that is required. As part of the programme, schools were given an audit tool and forms on which to record progress. The pilot of the project, which was written in 2018, featured the case study schools that took part, two of which are described after the conversation with Amelia.

### In conversation with Dr Amelia Roberts, Vice Dean Enterprise, Institute of Education, UCL discussing the SWERL Programme

**Q. Tell us about the background to SWERL.**

A. Our Knowledge Exchange Programmes (KEPs) enable us to work with schools in order to develop practice and improve outcomes for pupils, particularly those who are seen as vulnerable. Previous programmes have been Maximising the Impact of Teaching Assistants and Promoting the Achievement of Looked After Children. With all our programmes, we plan for them to have a continuous life, although that may mean the programme evolves over time. We support schools in identifying an area for change to improve their support of vulnerable pupils and support them with their action plan every step of the way.

**Q. What was the process for selecting schools?**

A.  We had an application process for the pilot and as we had more schools apply than we could accommodate, we went for a range of schools that were large enough to take this on and had a wider reach beyond their own provision. The majority of schools were new to us; only one or two had worked with us before.

**Q. Why was it important to use Kotter's eight-stage change model?**

A.  All our Knowledge Exchange Programmes have used Kotter's theory of change, as it is intuitive and provides a structure to help schools manage change with our facilitators' support, which is the way we prefer to work.

**Q. How did you decide on the seven domains you specified when working with this group of schools?**

A.  We created the seven domains after reviewing the literature. These are:

- Supported and informed staff
- Graduated Response to Need (role of the teacher)
- Enabling Environment
- Whole School Coherence and Design
- Building Relationships
- Robust Communication Systems
- Planning Transitions

(O'Brien and Roberts, 2019)

There was a debate about whether or not we should have a separate strand for pupil voice and for parents/carers, but we decided that these should run through everything rather than being seen as separate.

Although we are aware that some domains overlap or are interrelated, we wanted to make sure each one was sufficiently clearly defined to be useful to schools. The final one about transitions came in later when we realised how significant these were, from the micro level of changes within and between lessons, to the change caused by e.g., a bereavement. This proved useful in holding a magnifying glass to what was happening. For example, one school realised that 95% of incidents happened during the lunch break, so that became a major focus, and, once identified, could be addressed.

**Q. Schools are increasingly coming to the realisation that research- ers and practitioners benefit from sharing their knowledge. How would you sum up what the school's researchers gained from their involvement?**

A.  All our KEPs have a Review Day, when schools come to us to explain what occurred during the project, the outcomes that came from it and how they will use the knowledge they have gained to continue the work into the future. I always find these occasions provide a really rich engagement between practitioners and researchers.

The schools that gain the most are those who embed practice, for instance by setting up a Wellbeing Team or having a SWERL governor so that they revisit the Audit Tool on a regular basis and it becomes part of the ongoing School Improvement Plan.

From the point of view of the researchers, they felt they had made schools more comfortable with the idea of being involved in research and are clearer about how to analyse data and make use of it. For example, one school put up a sheet of A3 paper and asked everyone to write a Post-it note saying what they saw on the playground. Some wrote about particular children who stood out as being on their own or appearing to be unhappy, while others commented on the behaviour of certain individuals which opened up discussions about how the way children behaved linked to how they were feeling.

A second observation by the researchers was that they thought the tone of staffroom conversations changed, from being negative about the class they were about to teach or certain individuals in that class, to taking a more positive, problem-solving attitude, either by talking about how they were going to try a different approach, or asking colleagues for ideas about how they might come up with a solution together.

**Q.** **Have any adjustments or significant changes been made to SWERL in readiness for the next phase of the project?**

**A.** Although the model remains basically the same, it is being adapted to meet different situations. For instance, we've been invited to work with the Ipswich Opportunity Area. Part of our work will be to have a cohort of SWERL schools in Suffolk and develop leadership capacity to support sustainability, which will make an interesting contrast to working with schools in the London area.

To find another way of reaching schools beyond London, we are setting up a virtual SWERL programme, delivered online via a range of platforms.

**Q.** **Do you think a biopsychosocial model helps us to understand and support pupils with SEMH difficulties? If so, what might be its practical value for teachers?**

**A.** The theory is based on the work of John Morton and Uta Frith who wanted to look at the wider reasons for mental health and wellbeing using a causal modelling framework which was then set against a purely medical model. So each individual is seen as operating within their own social setting. Of course some conditions, such as schizophrenia or obsessive compulsive disorder (OCD), are likely to require some medical assistance, but adapting the environment and the context will meet the majority of needs.

For example, a boy in Year 1 found the transition from playtime to lessons really hard and his behaviour escalated at this point. The solution was to give him more support at these times, which also had the benefit of showing him that school is a place that cares about him. Or take the example of a BAME child who gets excluded for aggression because the member of staff misinterprets ways of behaving which are part of his culture. This fragments the relationship from the start and impacts on his resilience.

Q. **Are there any general approaches you believe should be included in a book on emotional wellbeing and mental health?**

A. I think that what is most helpful is to give links to charities who work in this field and who produce a range of resources, information and ideas for schools, such as Anna Freud's Schools in Mind, MindEd, YoungMinds, etc. In addition, there are other smaller charities who specialise in different conditions such as anxiety.

Q. **Is there anything else you would like to say about the value of SWERL?**

A. I believe that schools already have the answers, but someone from outside may help to bring them to the surface. For instance, a school may overlook the fact that if the same small group of pupils appear in detention every week, what needs to change may be the school's behaviour policy. Are detentions useful for all students, or might something else work better?

This is one of the strengths of a programme that has, for instance, researchers and practitioners working together, enabling someone from outside the situation to provide a fresh pair of eyes. Often, as Amelia points out, this can result in discovering that a school has the answer but needs time for reflection to reveal what it is.

### Case study of St Elizabeth Catholic School

The first school involved in the pilot was St Elizabeth Catholic School in London. The school chose the domains of Planning Transitions and Robust Communication Systems.

## Case study St Elizabeth Catholic School, Tower Hamlets

There were many different transitions staff were aware of that some pupils found difficult but when they looked into it more closely, the one causing the most difficulty, including for those with SEMH, were the Christmas festivities, which most children look forward to.

The school drew up an action plan for pupils in Y4 to buddy up with Y1 pupils, from the end of the autumn term to the start of the spring term. A robust communication project was devised for this project with a letter being sent to the parents of the children in both classes. Y4 pupils wrote to their Y1 buddies, as well, to introduce themselves. In December they wrote a second letter, saying they would think of them over Christmas and looked forward to seeing them again next term. The parents were also informed and asked to help their children read the letters. When the term started again, the buddies had another playtime together, having had one the previous term.

The outcome, as triangulated from Y1, Y4 and from parents/carers, has been that the buddy system has continued in the form of reading partners on a Friday afternoon. As it has helped the children involved to talk about responsibility, friendships and feelings, the pattern will continue with these and other groups as they move through the school, as well as a similar process being used in other situations.

The notion of having a buddy system for staff has been considered, particularly for those who are new to the school, while other schools have expressed an interest in using the buddy system as a template for supporting resilience in their own schools.

This was an example of a school giving time to focus on a particular issue, in this case planning transitions, and realising that a transition not previously considered was the need to help pupils who do not look forward to the Christmas festivities and all the changes that occur at this time. The school was also looking at improving communication and found a way of using pupils' writing to support both younger pupils and to involve parents.

### Case study of Furze Down School

The second case study school from the SWERL pilot is Furze Down, an all-age special school with a specialisation in communication and interaction. All pupils have speech, language and communication needs (SLCN); a significant majority have an ASD profile and often ASD/ADHD comorbidity; and increasing numbers have SEMH needs due to a variety of factors. The school is determined to promote positive mental health and is acutely aware of the correlation between SEND and increased vulnerability to compromised emotional wellbeing. As part of an Emotional Health and Wellbeing Team, the school has a Mindfulness Lead, who is trained to teach Paws b. Mindfulness is practised from early years to Key Stage 3 where the Paws b programme is embedded in the curriculum.

---

## Information point   Mindfulness

**Mindfulness** is about learning to live in the moment and to sustain attention, rather than let the mind wander, or worrying about the past or future.

**.b** mindfulness curriculum has been designed for secondary schools.

**Paws .b** introduces mindfulness to 7- to 11-year-olds through a series of sessions which are adapted from .b mindfulness secondary curriculum.

**Mindfulness in Schools Project** (MiSP) is a national, not-for-profit charity for young people and schools, which aims to make a positive difference to the wellbeing of pupils.

---

During the pilot year of the SWERL project, the school sought to establish a whole-school approach to mental health, emphasise the wellbeing of staff as a core focus, make early identification and intervention a priority, become an attachment-aware school, and equip pupils with skills to cope with change to reduce anxiety. The domains they chose were: Supported and informed staff; Graduated response to need; Building relationships.

## Case study   Furze Down School, Bucks

For the SWERL project, a multi-disciplinary team decided to pilot six interventions:

1   *Friends for life* (Paula Barrett), a resilience, social and emotional skills programme for children aged eight to eleven, which aims to prevent anxiety and has been recognised as effective by the World Health Organisation (WHO). A long-term plan was devised to run throughout Key Stages 3 and 4.

2   *Thinking together* (Neil Mercer), a University of Cambridge project promoting children's awareness of talk as a tool for thinking, so they not only interact but 'interthink'. Lessons were timetabled for collaborative work across the curriculum.

3   *Comic strip conversations* (Carol Gray), best known for her Social Stories, Gray has produced visual representations to help children understand what is involved in conversations.

4   *Zones of Regulation* (Leah M. Kuypers), a framework designed to foster self-regulation and emotional control using four coloured zones to describe different levels of emotion. This led to all staff being trained by OT/SaLT to deliver lessons across the schools.

> 5    *When the adult changes, everything changes* (Paul Dix), a book outlining five pillars of practice, based on consistency and certainty. A Book Club was established to become familiar with the ideas.
>
> 6    *Solution circles*, a creative problem-solving tool to build community capacity by working through a problem together. This resulted in INSET sessions being delivered so that more staff could become familiar with this approach.
>
> In addition to taking these interventions forward, the school agreed to have a mindfulness room for staff and pupils, to create more opportunities for pupils' ideas to be included in curriculum design and to appoint a trained mental health lead.

In addition, the school continued to make SEMH a top priority. Linked to Maslow's hierarchy of needs the school adapted the timetable to have class breakfast at the beginning of the day followed by a lesson with the tutor, giving pupils time to regulate their emotions and to have an opportunity to speak to key adults, if they needed to.

The school has continued to use the SWERL framework and is developing a bespoke curriculum for teaching about emotional health and wellbeing, building on the school's current SEMH curriculum. They are working to create a framework for assessing the quality and impact of the provision and increasing the opportunities for staff and pupils to develop resilience skills for self-actualisation.

## Statutory roles

Turning to roles that are statutory and may overlap with newer roles to do with mental health and wellbeing, are three roles that schools must have and which must be carried out by teachers who have had training for the role, namely:

- Special Educational Needs Co-ordinator (SENCO), which is sometimes referred to by a different name such as Inclusion Co-ordinator
- Designated safeguarding lead (DSL)
- Designated teacher for looked-after and previously looked-after children (LAC)

The latter role has been changed to include 'previously looked-after children' and guidance published by the DfE in 2018. The teacher carrying out this role will work closely with the virtual school head (VSH).

> ## Information point   Virtual schools and the VSH
>
> Since 2014, all LAs are required to appoint an officer for the position of virtual school head (VSH), to promote the educational attainment of looked-after children, who often have to change schools, and sometimes move to different families as well.
>
> Virtual schools are a concept whereby the pupils in an LA are treated as if they were all in the same 'virtual' school under a VSH. This model is not essential but is followed by most LAs.
>
> Designated teachers for LAC work closely with the VSH, in order to ensure that the progress of children involved is closely monitored even when their circumstances change.

### Designated teacher for LAC

Governors are responsible for making sure the head teacher, or a qualified teacher in the school, takes on this role in order to promote the educational achievement of looked-after pupils and previously looked-after children, who are no longer looked after in England or Wales because they are the subject of an adoption, special guardianship or child arrangements order, or were adopted from state care outside England or Wales. These pupils are eligible for Pupil Premium Plus (PP+) funding. The virtual school head (VSH) and the designated teacher need to work together to determine how the funding should be used to improve pupils' attainment.

As these children are more likely to have SEND than their peers, and, in particular, to have SEMH due in part to disruptions in their lives, the LAC and SENCO should work closely together and with the SMHL or strategic lead for mental health. One obvious example of this is making sure that the Personal Education Plan (PEP), which is part of a looked-after child's care plan, aligns with their EHCP if they have one.

### Designated safeguarding lead (DSL)

The DSL must be a senior member of the school's or college's leadership team, as they have the main responsibility for child protection issues in the school, including online safety. Their training should be updated every two years so that the latest child protection and safeguarding legislation and guidance is covered. The DSL should also undertake Prevent awareness training, which is designed to help staff protect pupils from the risk of being radicalised. It is part of the DSL's role to refer all cases of suspected abuse to the LA children's social care and, for any cases involving a member of staff, to the LA's designated officer (LADO).

The DfE's guidance is updated regularly and in the 2020 version, Annex B gives a full description of the role of the DSL which includes the following:

- Liaising with staff (especially pastoral support staff, school nurses, IT specialists and SENCOs or the named person with oversight for SEN in a college) on matters of safety and safeguarding (including online and digital safety) and then deciding whether to make a referral by liaising with relevant agencies
- Being able to recognise the additional risks that children with SEND face online, for example, from online bullying, grooming and radicalisation and are confident they have the capability to support SEND children to stay safe online

Again the need to work closely with the SENCO is underlined.

### SENCO/inclusion manager

It is a statutory requirement for all maintained schools to have a SENCO apart from special schools who can decide whether or not to have one. A very rough estimate suggests that around half of special schools have a SENCO to help with the strategic overview of a more complex population and about half take the view that, as all their pupils have SEND and an EHCP, responsibilities can be shared between staff. A SENCO must be a qualified teacher and achieve the National Award in Special Educational Needs Coordination (NASENCO) within three years of appointment.

As there is an overlap between the SENCO's role, in terms of SEMH being one of the four broad areas of need in the SEND Code of Practice, and the role of the person who has the strategic overview for pupils' mental health, there has sometimes been an assumption that the SENCO will cover both roles. In smaller schools this may be inevitable, as each member of staff, including the head teacher, will carry out many additional roles. In larger schools, where roles can be shared out, putting both roles under the same person endangers diluting these two strategic roles.

## Non-statutory and other roles

### Senior mental health lead (SMHL)

The role of the SMHL was outlined in the previous chapter and the point was made that, while not mandatory, schools are being encouraged to appoint someone to take the strategic overview of mental health in the school. Where a school is large enough to be able to appoint different people to the posts of SMHL, SENCO, DSL and LAC, they will need to work very closely together, with the responsibilities of each role being clearly delineated. Otherwise, they may be dealing with the same students but without sharing the information, while other students may fall through the gaps.

### Education mental health practitioner (EMHP)

The SMHL is the person who will be the school's main link with the EMHP. This role was also outlined in the previous chapter, together with the case study of Maple Primary School, which is involved in the Mental Health Trailblazer Programme. The following conversation is with Carolyn McKay, who is the EMHP at the school.

*In conversation with Carolyn McKay, EMHP, Hertfordshire*

**Q. Is your background in health, education, both, or something else?**

A. My degree is in Psychology with Criminology, which took me on to working in prevention at the Youth Offending Team. I then worked as an Intensive Family Support Worker, before training and working as a Primary School teacher. These skills were a good foundation for the role of EMHP.

**Q. How did you find the training for your role? Did it prepare you well?**

A. The training for the role was excellent. I trained at the Anna Freud Centre/ UCL. The clinical and education specialists taught me everything I needed to know about early prevention of mental health difficulties, using the manualised treatment methods and working with schools. It was hard work to juggle assignments with full-time study and work (along with two young children!) but it was incredibly interesting, rewarding and enjoyable. The assignments were practical and useful in providing the necessary experience for the role. The weeks at university consisted of lectures run by specialists in the field and a Practice Tutor Group where we were able to role play and embed the skills we were being taught.

**Q. How many schools and colleges do you cover and how much time can you give each one?**

A. I cover four schools; two primary, one secondary and one FE. During the training year, I had three days to work in schools (and two days at university). Since being qualified I have reduced my working hours to three days a week. This means the schools get approximately half a day each of my time, and the rest of the time is allocated for meetings, admin and supervision.

**Q. Could you describe your Mental Health Support Team (MHST)? How many EMHPs does it include and who else is part of the team?**

A. Currently, we are a team of four EMHPs plus one team leader, one administrator, and one clinical supervisor. We have a programme manager who is overseeing the set-up of MHSTs in Hertfordshire. We are in the process of recruiting a CWP (children's wellbeing practitioner) for the team as well. We did have an assistant psychologist who played a big part in setting up our systems for recording interventions and analysing data.

**Q.  How would you describe your role in schools? How much does it vary depending on the nature of the different schools on your patch and what they need?**

A.  Our role is to provide early intervention to children and young people experiencing low-level mental health difficulties. It is a brief (about eight weeks) solution-focused intervention that uses the principles of Cognitive Behaviour Therapy. It is a guided self-help approach, so we work collaboratively with parents and young people to develop strategies to manage their anxiety or low mood.

In primary schools, we work with parents as we believe they know their child best and evidence shows that giving parents the strategies of how to support their children will have a longer-term impact. We have two interventions; one is for parents of children who have some low-level anxiety and one is for parents of children younger than 9, who display some low-level challenging behaviour.

We also run an eight-week group for primary school children in Key Stage 2, called Brain Buddies. The course aims to develop students' understanding of what emotion regulation is. This is done via skills building in understanding, identifying and developing strategies for regulating their emotions through self-care, self-calming strategies and thinking strategies such as problem-solving.

In secondary and FE sites, we work one-to-one with adolescents who are experiencing some low-level anxiety or low mood. We can also work with groups of young people, following a programme of Interpersonal Psychotherapy for Adolescents (IPT-A) which supports young people experiencing low mood in recognising how their relationships affect their mood and to work on communication strategies.

We work closely with the mental health leads of schools, offer staff workshops and support the school with their whole-school approach to mental health and wellbeing. We offer workshops for young people on, for example, transitions or exam stress. We also offer workshops to parents on, for example, managing children's anxiety or supporting their child's emotional regulation. In this respect, our work will vary depending on what the school needs.

**Q  Do you meet with EMHPs from different MHSTs?**

A.  We haven't formally met other MHSTs. We frequently liaise with the MHST in East Herts and have worked more closely during this period of remote working to cover the workload across Hertfordshire. Informally, we speak with colleagues we trained with, who are working in MHSTs across London, to share resources and ideas.

**Q. Do you have ongoing training and/or supervision?**

A. Yes, we are able to access regular training as required. For example, we have received some training on supporting young people with autism.

We have regular supervision. We have clinical supervision fortnightly and line management supervision monthly. We also have group supervision monthly.

**Q. Do you have a direct link with CAMHS if necessary? Do they still talk in terms of a four-tiered approach?**

A. We are part of one CAMHS service but we are based in schools, rather than clinics. Our Team Leader attends the quadrant team meetings and can take any cases we want to discuss with the MDT for them to take on, and they can offer some support. Although we still talk in terms of 'four tiers', there is a move towards the Thrive Framework now for the delivery of mental health services.

## Making the most of existing expertise

In addition to the roles already described, it is important to consider the contributions that other staff may be able to make, while being aware of any addition to their workload. Who these people are will vary considerably. Some schools may be able to appoint their own educational psychologist (EP), therapists, counsellors or mentors; others may share them with another school; or they will not be members of staff as such, but come in to deliver sessions. In some settings, governors may play a role and that can be helpful to raise the profile.

The list that follows is not hierarchical. The SMHL is placed at the top because this is the person who has the strategic overview.

**Senior mental health lead** (SMHL)

**EMHP SENCO, DSL** and **LAC**

Head or Co-ordinator PSHE      Pastoral Lead/tutor/class teacher

Staff with relevant training e.g., The Link Project, MHFA, etc.

EP, therapists, counsellors, mentors

All staff (and governors)

## Behaviour policies and principles

Although schools are required to have both a Behaviour Policy and a Behaviour Principles Written Statement – which can be one document – they are not required, at present, to have a Mental Health Policy, although some schools have decided to have one.

### Case study of Springhallow School

An example of this is Springhallow School in Ealing, London, which is a maintained school for pupils aged 4 to 16 years, who have an EHCP specifying that they have a diagnosis of autism. In September 2019, the school opened a Post-16 provision.

The school's core values are expressed as:

- *A*ccepting
- *U*nderstanding
- *T*ogether
- *I*ndividual
- *S*upportive
- *M*utual respect

The school has an eclectic approach to teaching pupils with autism and uses elements of ABA (Applied Behaviour Analysis), PBS (Positive Behaviour Support), TEACCH (Treatment and Education of Autistic and Communication Handicapped Children) and the use of Makaton and PECS (Picture Exchange Communication System) to enhance pupils' access to language.

One of the school's main aims is to foster 'Positive Wellbeing' and to make sure this has a recognised role within the school. There is a clear Positive Mental Health Policy, which is updated annually. The case study that follows gives an idea of its contents.

## Case study   Springhallow School's Positive Mental Health Policy

After a short introduction, which includes the World Health Organisation (WHO) definition of mental health (as quoted in the opening chapter of this book) the policy is set out as follows:

**Aims**   Promoting positive mental health; increasing awareness of common mental health issues; alerting staff to early warning signs and giving them support when working with young people who have mental health issues; providing knowledge and support to pupils who have mental health needs, their peers and parents or carers

**Lead members of staff**   While the policy makes clear that all staff have a responsibility to promote the mental health of students, staff with a specific remit are listed as:

- Designated safeguarding lead (DSL)
- Mental health lead (MHL)
- Mental health first aider (MHFA)
- CPD lead
- Head of PSHE

**Teaching about mental health**   The PSHE Association Guidance is followed to ensure mental health and emotional wellbeing are taught in a safe and sensitive manner. (There is more about the PSHE Association materials in Chapter 5 of this book.)

**Signposting**   Staff, students and parents are made aware of sources of support within the school and in the local community.

**Warning signs**   A list of warning signs is given that might indicate a student is having mental health or emotional wellbeing issues.

**Managing disclosures** and **confidentiality**   Clear procedures are laid out about what to do in these situations.

**Working with parents** and **training**   The importance of keeping parents informed and working with them in supporting children who have mental health issues is stressed.

**Training**   The need for all staff to receive regular training and those who need more in-depth knowledge will be discussed as part of the performance management process.

The school has a dog called Jess, who is a registered PaT (Pets as Therapy) dog, which means she has received training to carry out her role within the school.

Springhallow also runs an Outreach Service, which is commissioned by Ealing LA and supports local primary and secondary schools through visits and offering training. This is delivered to early years, schools and Post-16 provision, using the Autism Education Trust (AET) materials. The AET is a partnership between Ambitious About Autism (AAA), Autism Alliance (an organisation that brings autism charities together), and the National Autistic Society (NAS). The training materials have been developed with support from the DfE.

The final conversation in this chapter is with Penny Broadhurst, who is a social worker by training, but who has, for many years, been an assistant head whose role includes wellbeing. The success of the moves to establish emotional wellbeing more firmly in schools may depend on professionals from different backgrounds working and training together more closely so that children and young people are viewed in the round.

*In conversation with Penny Broadhurst, Assistant Head (Wellbeing)*

**Q. How did you start working in schools? What are your responsibilities as an assistant head (wellbeing)?**

A. I've had 20 years working in social care starting off in child protection and safeguarding. When the opportunity arose to work with a group of schools on a deprived housing estate, I realised the gap there was sometimes between home and school, so I developed a team of home/school link workers, using staff who were already in schools, but changing their roles.

In 2001, the area where I was working became an Education Action Zone and for seven years, I helped to co-ordinate the work by creating a Family Support Team. This led to the Hampshire Early Years Hub, which looks at referrals and tries to improve early intervention. Parents and children are involved. I believe that it is important to start by gaining the trust of parents. All this experience helped me when I moved to working full-time in a school. This was Prospect School, which is for secondary-aged boys who have social, emotional and behavioural difficulties (SEBD).

One of my first moves was to pull together a Wellbeing Team so that all the staff concerned with pupils' wellbeing knew what each other was doing and could share their knowledge and expertise. As an assistant head, I also developed the school's Outreach Service, giving it the name 'Include'. Schools pay to have the service which includes mentoring young people.

My role as an assistant head is a pastoral one, monitoring the work of the Wellbeing Team, which the other two social workers run. I have responsibility for safeguarding and child protection. Part of my role is also to have oversight of the interventions that are being used and to monitor how effective they are. It also ensures that some pupils aren't receiving too many interventions while others fall through the gaps.

**Q. Do you supervise social work students both at the school and elsewhere?**

A. Yes, I work with University of Portsmouth over placing social work trainees and supervising them, both at Prospect School and in other settings, including mainstream schools. As this has been going for some time, I've been able employ two of them who have since qualified and are now part of 'Include'. I think outreach work helps with early identification. Why wait for children to fail before someone does something about it?

**Q. Could you describe your Wellbeing Team and how it came together?**

A. When I arrived at the school, there were several teaching assistants who had various roles, but they worked separately from each other, so I pulled them together to form a Wellbeing Team. A counsellor I'd worked with before joined the team and any trainee social workers became part of it. It took four or five years before the work of the team was embedded in the school. This includes having written referrals from form tutors, who work with parents in filling in the forms before sending them to the Team. Once the Wellbeing Team has decided what is needed, the tutor, family and pupil still remain involved. This ensures that everyone knows their roles and works together to solve a problem. The Wellbeing Team also works with siblings whose difficulties sometimes get overlooked.

**Q. How much of your role is with staff and governors as well as pupils and families?**

A. Governors take a keen interest in what is happening and receive termly reports.

Circle time is used with staff and is based on the one-to-five scale of solution-focused brief therapy. This involves team building with six to eight staff at a time, when we discuss how we're feeling and share ideas. The Wellbeing Team is there for all staff as well as pupils and families When we had a problem with pupil attendance, the team met with tutors and together devised a reward system that worked.

**Q. Tell us about some of the approaches or interventions the school uses to support wellbeing.**

A. Some of the boys could be resistant to the idea of seeing a counsellor but responded better to having a mentor. This was a one-to-one adult who took a solution-focused approach to their informal sessions, which might take place while going for a walk, playing a board game or having lunch together. These sessions became so popular that we had to cut down on the number of sessions they could have.

There needs to be a menu so that interventions can be matched to the pupil. We do use Restorative Justice and we have two emotional literacy support assistants (ELSAs). Sometimes they work with a pupil who isn't prepared to have counselling but later may be ready to take this step. The Wellbeing Team meets monthly to check whether the interventions are working. For parents, we use Family Therapy and Family Group Conferencing.

**Q. What outside agencies do you link with and have you been involved in the Mental Health Trailblazer Programme at all?**

A. I've met three of the local EMHPs, but they are still in training. They seem to use mostly cognitive behaviour therapy (CBT).

We have half termly surgeries with each of our outreach schools where they have a day or half day as part of their fee. We discuss any pupils who are of concern and make sure they do some of the work as well as having the team's support. Parents are included in 'Include' from the start.

We also meet the Youth Offending Team (YOT) and share information if we're working with the same pupils.

**Do you offer training either inside or beyond the school?**

A. Yes, CAMHS often provide materials or will come themselves. We also train our staff and the schools where we do outreach. When working with parents, much of it is about increasing tolerance and having strategies to enable this to happen.

**Q. Is there anything else that might be of interest to readers or you would like to mention?**

A. Throughout my career I've been involved in supervision. I think it's very important for staff to have the opportunity to reflect on what has happened and what might be the next steps. I would like it to be seen as normal for staff to receive counselling as well as the pupils.

While few schools may be in a position to replicate this model, co-ordinating the work that goes on in a school or college in whatever way is possible and helpful is something that needs to be considered.

In the final case study in this chapter, there is a reference to using SEAL. Interestingly enough, this programme was established long before there was such an emphasis on emotional wellbeing in schools and other settings. The school also adapts the Zones of Regulation for the different age groups.

## Information point   Social and Emotional Aspects of Learning (SEAL)

SEAL was piloted by the government as far back as 2004. The following year, the materials were made available to all primary schools in England to be used with 3- to 11-year-olds. Later, it was rolled out to secondary schools for 11- to 16-year-olds and included a range of web-based materials.

SEAL aims to support children and young people in developing the personal and social skills of:

- Self-awareness
- Managing feelings
- Motivation
- Empathy
- Social skills

These interpersonal and intrapersonal skills have been shown to improve learning and promote emotional health and wellbeing. SEAL can be used by whole classes, small groups, and for intensive individual support.

## Information point   Zones of regulation

This is a framework to foster self-regulation and emotional control. The zones are based on a cognitive-behavioural approach which sets out to teach students to become aware of their emotions so that they can learn to be more in control of them.

Three of the four zones are the same as the traffic light system.

*Red zone* which describes a state of heightened alertness and intense emotions, such as anger, rage, intense sadness or terror.

*Yellow zone* is used to describe heightened states of alertness and elevated emotions, such as stress, frustration, anxiety, excitement or nervousness, but a person has greater control over them.

*Green zone* is used to describe a calm state of alertness, which includes being happy or content and is a good state to be in for learning.

*Blue zone* describes a low state of alertness, when there is a feeling of apathy, sadness, tiredness or boredom.

### Case study of Highbury Infants & Nursery School and Whitehill JM

The final case study is about an Infant & Nursery School and a Junior School in Hitchin, Hertfordshire. They do not share the same site, but are geographically close. A member of the SLT leads on Inclusion and Wellbeing in both schools. Both schools place an emphasis on the wellbeing of pupils, their families and staff, and being aware that anxious, sad or confused pupils find it hard to concentrate on learning.

## Case study   Highbury Infant & Nursery School and Whitehill Junior School

The head teachers, Helen Avey (Highbury) and Steve Mills (Whitehill) are clear that wellbeing is not something that can be covered or fixed in a year, but that it is a question of embedding good practice so that it will become a life skill that is every bit as important as learning to read, write and calculate.

In terms of wellbeing, the aims for both schools are as follows:

- For children to develop academic and emotional resilience through having access to pastoral and intervention support, leading to an increase in their mental wellbeing and happiness. Resilience is articulated and rewarded, in order to help children cope with the ups and downs of life
- For staff to feel encouraged and supported and to ensure that work is a place of safety and happiness, where they are pleased to be. Report writing has been reviewed with the aim of reducing workload, while 'feel good' incentives, such as biscuit briefings, strawberry staff meetings and pamper evenings are going to be increased
- For parents to feel they are supported, listened to, and informed about good mental health so that they can support their own wellbeing and that of their children.

Both schools use the NHS 'Five ways to wellbeing' (NHS, 2019) so that children are taught both the academic and emotional skills they need to feel good, now and as they get older. There are displays about each of the Five Ways in classrooms as well as centrally, which act as constant reminders that everyone can be in charge of their own feelings and wellbeing.

Parents have been encouraged to use the Five Ways as well, both for their own wellbeing and that of their children. Staff and parents have received workshops giving them ideas about how to put them into practice.

At Highbury, the school's 'Policy for Promoting Positive Behaviour' begins with a reminder that everyone in the school community is 'entitled to respect, self-esteem and the opportunity to develop self-reliance'. There is an emphasis on noticing and rewarding good behaviour. Class circle time is used to resolve class issues. Where sanctions are necessary, these include 'reflection time', when a child is taken away from the class and a sand timer shows the length of time before rejoining the group. There is a 'quiet space' for children who need space and peace at playtimes and a 'Circle of Friends' group for those who struggle to form friendships.

Highbury has a Wellbeing Governor, who collects views from children about how safe and secure they feel in school. At Whitehill, there is a 'calm down' space with sensory toys, and a number of groups address different needs. These include:

- Totally Topical – to give children a chance to increase their sense of self-worth by being able to shine at something they choose and enjoy
- Confident Kids – to increase the confidence of girls and to enable them to form a relationship with a trusted adult
- Mindful Boys – to help them focus, feel calmer and learn mindfulness techniques to use at other times
- Yoga and aromatherapy taster sessions.

SEAL is used to support the development of personal and social skills; 'Protective Behaviours' work is timetabled so that it is revisited termly; and the Zones of Regulation have been modified in line with the age and stage of the children, to help pupils to understand their feelings and how to regulate them.

Before a conversation with the inclusion/wellbeing lead for both schools, Steve Mills, head teacher of Whitehill JM, explained how 'Profound Individual Growth' came to describe the school's core purpose:

> During my first year as head, I worked on our vision. I read Simon Sinek's (2011) book, which suggests starting with 'Why' rather than 'What', e.g. not *what* we do but *why* we do it. I worked with one of my governors (who happens to be a marketing guru) to simplify the ideas into three words, hence 'Profound Individual Growth'. Basically, it means making each person a better version of themselves. It's not all about English and Maths, but could equally mean a better athlete, linguist, or artist. Our slogan is: 'Working Together for Individual Success'.

Perhaps it is the ability of these two schools to work together that enabled Antonia to carry out a role that would normally be split between two or more people.

*In conversation with Antonia McConnell Smith, Inclusion and Wellbeing Lead*

**Q. How do you manage to divide your time as Assistant Head and Inclusion/Wellbeing Lead at two schools?**

A. Technically, I work two days for each school. I try and work the first two at Highbury Infants and then Wednesdays and Thursdays at Whitehill JM. However, the key to the success of this set-up is in the flexibility and trust from both head teachers and in being a senior leader in both schools. My role as Inclusion Lead, includes (amongst others): the SENCO role, dDSL, Wellbeing/Mental Health Lead, including the mentoring involved.

The illusion is that both schools get four days of attention, responses and work from me. Although during the time I am physically in one of the settings, I will of course be doing the stuff that needs to be done, such as screening and observations, liaising with staff and external agencies, progress meetings etc. The rest of the time, emails, resources, phone calls and so on can be done anywhere. This means that things can be dealt with in a timely manner. One of the key ingredients to having happy children is having happy adults and as such responding to parents or staff as soon as an issue arises for them (or us!).

Both heads are happy to let me decide where to spend time and see the joint outcome as beneficial. For example, I will move between schools to accommodate visits from external professionals so that we have maximum flexibility and can respond swiftly. The same with parent meetings, family support workers, the virtual school, etc. Basically, if my changing makes it better for one setting and does not disadvantage the other, then I will make myself available. Working this way allows the two settings to become closer, which is of course good for children's outcomes. We now share many initiatives and each setting has a better understanding of the challenges faced by the other.

Both schools will be introducing Jigsaw (the PHSE programme) this year. Safeguarding and some other training is done together. Initiatives such as the 'Five ways to wellbeing' or 'Zones of regulation' are introduced in both schools. Parent meetings are often offered to both schools and hosted in one or the other. Simply put, by working this way, we double the impact for our children and families. We are more available and responsive and can offer more in other ways, such as doubling training by splitting the bill, etc.

**Q. Are you currently using both Jigsaw and SEAL?**

A. We have bought into Jigsaw as a resource for delivering our RHE curriculum. Although this has been delayed until summer 2021, we are going to start the scheme now to ensure coverage and continuity in the future. I think it is a very comprehensive scheme – quite expensive, but worth it!

**Q. Is there a Wellbeing Wall and Worry Box in both schools?**

A. Not exactly. The basic principles are shared by both schools but due to ages and stages, they are treated differently. There *is* a Wellbeing Wall in each but the writing prowess of the infants makes the box not so handy. 'Feel good 5' at Whitehill became the 'Feel good fingers' at Highbury

**Q. There's a very informative PowerPoint presentation on your website for an Emotional Wellbeing Workshop for parents. Is this a one-off or a regular event?**

A. Workshops occur every year. The 'Five ways to wellbeing' was to be a termly event as we wanted to share the concepts so that parents could triangulate this good practice at home, but sadly we had COVID on the horizon and so did not get to do another this year. In the past we have had parent sessions on anxiety, resilience or other areas of interest to parents. We ask what they want and try to deliver it!

I always say that my core starting point is that happy children learn. The key for our schools, though, does not always lie in starting with the children, but in backtracking to the home. Much work therefore needs to be done in getting happy adults around them (parents and staff) as fundamentally this makes such a difference to the children's messages of security. If, where possible, we can work with parents to genuinely hear their fears, concerns and also provide positive feedback, then we have a good starting place for a solid relationship that is felt by the children, too. Sharing this ethos across both schools further adds to the feeling of safety by parents, teachers and children that we are in this together, not always getting it right but doing our best! Wellbeing is a particular passion of mine.

## Conclusions

The nature of mental health and emotional wellbeing means that everyone involved with young people, their families and, indeed, the whole of a community, might consider how to draw together the knowledge that exists already, as well as considering previously untapped sources of support. The creation of newer roles provides an opportunity to think about how to meld these newer roles with existing ones and to be open to different ways of working.

The next chapter moves on to look at the risk and protective factors in children's lives and what can be done to make all young people more resilient.

## References

Bowlby, J. (1944) Forty-four juvenile thieves: Their characters and home-life. *International Journal of Psycho-Analysis*, 25, 107–128. Abingdon: Taylor and Francis (International).

Central Advisory Council for Education (1967) *Children and Their Primary Education: The Plowden Report*. London: HMSO.

Cole, J. (Editor) *Nebraska Symposium in Motivation, 1971.* Vol. 19. Lincoln: University of Nebraska Press.

Colley, D. and Cooper, P. (2017) *Attachment and Emotional Development on the Classroom p27.* London: Jessica Kingsley Publishing.

DfE (2016) *Behaviour and Discipline in Schools.* Available from https://assets.publishing.service.gov.uk/government/uploads/system/uploads/attachment_data/file/488034/Behaviour_and_Discipline_in_Schools_-_A_guide_for_headteachers_and_School_Staff.pdf

DfE (2018) *The Designated Teacher for Looked after and previously Looked after Children.* Available from https://assets.publishing.service.gov.uk/government/uploads/system/uploads/attachment_data/file/683561/The_designated_teacher_for_looked-after_and_previously_looked-after_children.pdf

DfE (2020) *Keeping Children Safe in Education: Statutory Guidance for Schools and Colleges.* Available from https://assets.publishing.service.gov.uk/government/uploads/system/uploads/attachment_data/file/912592/Keeping_children_safe_in_education_Sep_2020.pdf

Goleman, D. (1996) *Emotional Intelligence.* London: Bloomsbury Publishing.

Goleman, D. (2007) *Social Intelligence.* London: Bloomsbury Publishing.

https://mindfulnessinschools.org/about/

Kotter, J. P. (1996) *Leading Change.* Boston: Harvard Business Review Press.

Maslow, A. H. (1943) A theory of human motivation. *Psychological Review*, 50(4), 370–396. Washington, DC: American Psychological Association.

Morgan, Dr R. OBE. Children's Rights Director for England (2014) *The Children's Happiness Scale.* Available from https://assets.publishing.service.gov.uk/government/uploads/system/uploads/attachment_data/file/379265/The_20Children_27s_20Happiness_20Scale.pdf

New Economics Foundation (2009) *A Guide to Measuring Children's Wellbeing.* Available from https://neweconomics.org/uploads/files/094c9bd92c79f7129f_w5m6i2zzh.pdf

NHS (2019) *5 Steps to Mental Well Being.* London: NHS. Available from www.nhs.uk/conditions/stress-anxiety-depression/improve-mental-wellbeing/

O'Brien, T. and Roberts, A. (2019) *A domains-based approach to meeting social, emotional and mental health needs.* Available from https://onlinelibrary.wiley.com/doi/abs/10.1111/1467-9604.12247

O'Regan, F. (2006) *Can't Learn, Won't Learn, and Those Who Simply Don't Care Whether They Learn or Not.* London: Bloomsbury Group.

Rogers, C. P. (1961) *On Becoming a Person: A Therapist's View of Psychotherapy.* Boston: Mariner Books.

Sinek, S. (2011) *Start with Why.* London: Penguin Group.

www.jigsawpshe.com

www.mindfulnessinschools.org

www.zonesofregulation.com

# Chapter 4

# Resilience
## Risk and protective factors

The time we are living in is sometimes referred to as the Fourth Industrial Revolution. There is a common theme among each of the industrial revolutions, which is the invention of a specific technology that changed society fundamentally. The first brought in the invention of the steam engine and mechanised the textile industry. The second heralded the age of electricity enabling mass production. The third saw the rise of electronics, telecommunications and, of course, computers. The present one is about smart technologies and everything being automated and connected.

In June 2019, the Department for Business, Energy and Industrial Strategy (BEIS) presented a policy to paper to Parliament which in the introduction said:

> The Fourth Industrial Revolution is of a scale, speed and complexity that is unprecedented. It is characterised by a fusion of technologies – such as artificial intelligence, gene editing and advanced robotics – that is blurring the lines between the physical, digital and biological worlds. It will disrupt nearly every industry in every country, creating new opportunities and challenges for people, places and businesses to which we must respond.
>
> (2019: 2)

Looking back, it is apparent that the gap between revolutions has been decreasing. In fact, some people are already talking about a fifth industrial revolution. Exacerbating the rate and amount of change, in 2020 COVID-19 hit countries across the world, accelerating societal changes at a rate no one could have envisaged. The point of all this is to suggest that, at a time when change is increasing so dramatically, the need for resilience has never been greater. It was mentioned in the opening chapter that today's society looks very different in terms of family structures, as the web of connections people used to create around them have been largely disrupted by the ease with which people can travel to different towns, cities and countries. This chapter will consider how to help younger generations become more resilient, but first some thoughts on what is meant by resilience.

# Resilience

Being resilient is not about sailing serenely through life unaffected by stress or misfortune, it is about the ability to withstand adversity and bounce back from difficult life events. Part of this is an ability to adjust to change. Resilient people do not dwell on failures; they acknowledge the situation, learn from their mistakes – if indeed mistakes were made – and then move on. Thomas Edison, the American inventor, is often held up as an example of being a resilient person in his search for a light bulb that worked. Building on the attempts of other inventors, he is said to have made literally thousands of prototypes, but he looked on each attempt as a step on the road to ultimate success. It is claimed that he said: 'I have not failed. I've just found 10,000 ways that won't work'. There is a lesson here in helping children not to be afraid of having a go because they think what matters is getting it right the first time they try to master a new skill.

Factors that have been identified as contributing towards being resilient include:

- Having the capacity to make realistic plans and to carry out those plans
- Being able to manage strong feelings and impulses
- Having good communication skills
- Having strong relationships
- Having effective problem-solving skills
- Having a positive self-image and confidence in one's own strengths and abilities

Many people have highlighted the concept of resilience as a relevant theme in education and its importance has grown at a time of unprecedented change. In a report by the Public Policy Institute for Wales which looked at promoting emotional health, wellbeing and resilience in primary schools, researchers from the University of Sussex commented that:

> Emotional health, mental health, well-being, resilience and life satisfaction are all broad headings that encompass a wide variety of phenomena that are emotional (e.g. feelings of anxiety), cognitive (e.g. beliefs about oneself), behavioural (e.g. participation in risky and/or antisocial behaviours), motivational (e.g. being able to bounce back from failure in order to work towards goals) and/or social-relational (e.g. positive relationships with others) (DfE et al., 2011; https://bounceforward.com/healthy-minds-research-project/).
>
> (Public Policy Institute for Wales, 2016: 6)

While it is clear that some young people are naturally more resilient than others, and some have received more than their fair share of setbacks, there is an acknowledgement that, at least to some extent, the skills of being resilient can be taught. As a result, a growing number of books, resources and programmes have sprung up to support those working in education to promote resilience in their students. While it is not possible to cover everything that is available, the following describes three that have had strong support and clear rationales.

### The UK Resilience Programme (UKRP)

UKRP aims to improve children's psychological wellbeing and build resilience. The programme is based on the USA's Penn Resiliency Program (https://ppc.sas.upenn.edu/research/resilience-children). Three LAs trialled UKRP in 2007–2008 for Year 7 pupils in secondary schools. The final evaluation of the programme appeared in 2011 as a DfE Research Report and found that the programme had a positive effect, including having a greater impact for the most vulnerable groups. Since then, some of the original schools have gone on to offer workshops to subsequent cohorts of pupils, and some have had additional staff members trained in teaching the programme. Although not all the original schools may continue to use it, other schools have started using the programme.

### The Resilience Framework

This framework was developed from a set of ideas by Angie Hart and Derek Blincow as part of a book they wrote about Resilient Therapy. The ideas have been built on to produce a 'Resilience Framework', in conjunction with the University of Brighton's Centre of Resilience for Social Justice, where Hart and Blincow are based. This is also the home of 'Boingboing', a Community Interest Company (CIC), which works in collaboration with service users, parents, young people and practitioners to bring together research, education and practice around resilience (Blincow et al., 2016).

The Resilience Framework fits neatly onto one side of A4 and, at first glance, the amount of information it contains is not apparent. There are five columns in different colours headed:

| | |
|---|---|
| **Basics** | Sorting out the basics such as being safe, having a healthy diet, exercising, having enough sleep, play and leisure, etc. |
| **Belonging** | Good relationships being at the heart of everything |
| **Learning** | The importance of finding out and constantly discovering new things |
| **Coping** | Strategies for self-help or for getting help when needed |
| **Core self** | Putting the focus on the thoughts and beliefs which build character |

Underneath each of these headings, however, is a series of subheadings which list the areas that may need further development. The interactive version of this framework enables the reader to point to any of these subheadings in order to gain access to a series of strategies to tackle the issue. This turns a single page resource into a mine of easily accessible information. The Resilience

Framework has been translated into many languages including: Danish, French, German, Greek, Italian, Norwegian, Polish, Portuguese and Spanish.

### Healthy Minds

The charity 'Bounce Forward' (previously known as 'How to Thrive'), researched a resilience-based PSHE curriculum with 11,000 students over five years. The evaluation showed largely positive results. 'Healthy Minds' is a four-year curriculum for Years 7 to 10. For each lesson there are detailed teaching and learning resources, written support for teachers, as well as training. Topics include: emotional resilience, mental health, social media, mindfulness, career hopes and human connection. The materials have been updated to cover health education (including teaching mental resilience), which became statutory beginning in September 2020. The whole of the Healthy Minds curriculum reflects the teachings of Positive Psychology, as it concentrates on building strengths, rather than focusing on weaknesses, and on what it is worth doing, rather than on what to avoid. (There is more about RSHE and ways of teaching these subjects in the next chapter.)

## Risk and protective factors

It was the psychiatrist Michael Rutter who in 1987 promoted the idea that there were risk factors and protective factors that could affect children's development. He described protective factors as being able to help mitigate the risks while promoting resilience. He noted that children respond to events differently due to their susceptibility to risk, and whether or not there are protective mechanisms coming into play to reduce the risks. Rutter built on Bowlby's work on attachment (mentioned in the previous chapter), by studying the fate of young children in Romanian orphanages and the long-term effects this had even when their care and surroundings improved dramatically.

The 'Mentally Healthy Schools' website points out that risks come in many forms and they may be linked to differences in a child's temperament, as well as the result of what they have experienced. Risk and protective factors are both set out under the four headings:

- In the child
- In the family
- In the school
- In the community

On the website, it suggests that it is helpful to think in terms of a Mental Health spectrum:

Healthy          Coping          Struggling          Unwell

And *where* a child is on the spectrum will depend on the complex relationship between their genetic make-up, external risks that jeopardise their social and emotional development, and the protective factors that can shield them from these risks. It points out that how the adults in children's lives take action to offset the family and environmental factors that undermine children's ability to flourish can make a substantial difference (www.mentallyhealthyschools.org.uk).

These same four categories are used in the DfE's advice for schools, when it says:

> Research suggests that there is a complex interplay between the risk factors in children's lives and the protective factors that are needed to act as a counterbalance. The key protective factors which build resilience to mental health problems are shown alongside the risk factors.
>
> (DfE, 2018: 13)

This is followed by risk and protective factors being set out under the four headings used on the 'Mentally Healthy Schools' website. Set out in this way, it is clear that some of these factors lie outside the influence of the school, or its influence can only be indirect. Taking each of these in turn can help to build up a picture of what educational settings can and cannot do to support the development of resilience in their students.

### Factors within the child

As has been mentioned before, some children have an innate ability to be more resilient and to bounce back from experiences or events that leave others struggling to cope. Their genetic predisposition enables them to take events or circumstances in their stride which others may find overwhelming. A child who is naturally resilient will cope better with additional difficulties, such as having SEND, being ill, or not doing well at school, whereas in other children their lack of resilience will make it harder for them to overcome any extra difficulties. Although the genetic make-up of a child cannot be changed, schools have a role in boosting pupils' resilience skills, both through the environment they create and through direct teaching. This will benefit all pupils but be of particular value to those who are not resilient by nature or whose negative experiences have taken too great a toll.

### Factors in the family

Although there is clearly a limit as to how far educational settings can influence the home, in recent years there has been much more of a focus on working in partnerships with parents. In a publication by Public Health England (PHE), which was also mentioned in the opening chapter, it states:

> The family plays a key role in influencing children and young people's emotional health and wellbeing. There is strong evidence that well

implemented universal and targeted interventions supporting parenting and family life that offer a combination of emotional, parenting and practical life circumstances (combining drug, alcohol and sex education, for example) have the potential to yield social as well as economic benefits.

(2015: 20)

Most parents and carers provide a supportive environment in which children can grow and flourish. This stable start will give them the protective factors that will stand them in good stead as they move through life. However, some families are unable to supply the nurturing children need. Far from providing a secure environment where the child can form an affectionate bond with at least one caregiver, the family itself leads to risk factors for the child. These may stem from parental conflict and family breakdown; physical, sexual or emotional abuse or neglect; inconsistent relationships and boundaries for the child; or parents being weighed down and wrestling with their own problems of alcoholism, drug misuse or mental illness.

Schools have changed over many years from keeping parents at the school gates to welcoming them in as partners in their child's education. Establishing good relationships, where pupils can see home and school working together, is one of the most positive developments a school can achieve. For some families, more support will be needed and many schools will either run parenting classes or link parents to courses they feel would be helpful.

### The Solihull Approach

This is an example of a programme that was established 20 years ago. It has also been used in other countries, such as Pakistan, Iceland, Australia, Ghana and Barbados. The model combines three theoretical concepts:

- Containment (psychoanalytic theory)
- Reciprocity (child development)
- Behaviour management (behaviourism)

It provides a framework for thinking for a wide range of professionals working with families, children and young people. Containment and reciprocity underpin relationships and brain development as well as the quality of an attachment. The Solihull Approach is included in the UK DoH's 'Healthy Child Programme', in Northern Ireland's strategy for training health visitors and midwives, and in Scotland's strategy for training health visitors and child practitioners. The approach aims to increase emotional health and wellbeing through reaching both practitioners and parents. In terms of schools, whole-school training for everyone from the school receptionists to teachers, support staff and governors is available.

The 'Solihull Approach Parenting Group', (also known as 'Understanding Your Child's Behaviour') is a universal parenting intervention for any parent with a child who has universal or complex needs between the ages of 0 and 18 (https://solihullapproachparenting.com).

## Factors in the school

It has become apparent through this and previous chapters that schools can be a positive or negative experience for pupils or, in most cases, a mixture of the two. Sometimes the school years cause feelings and emotions that can last a lifetime. In addition, schools are dealing with pupils who have had a range of experiences and – although this may not be a totally new phenomenon – changes in family structures and in society. This, in addition to the pressure on schools to produce academic outcomes, has presented teachers with classes that have a wide range of needs. For example, in the PHE document mentioned previously it was estimated that in an average class of thirty 15-year-old pupils:

- Three could have a mental disorder
- Ten are likely to have witnessed their parents separate
- One could have experienced the death of a parent
- Seven are likely to have been bullied
- Six may be self-harming

(2015: 5)

The main way in which schools can support their pupils' emotional health and wellbeing is to find ways of making them more resilient. This will be of benefit to all pupils, with special attention on those who have low wellbeing because of some of the factors described previously. In addition to this list, having some form of peer-to-peer support can be very beneficial.

### Peer-to-peer support

There have been some very successful examples of peer-to-peer support, where even quite young pupils have been trained to support their peers and to help them, for instance, to form friendships. In the Future in Mind document discussed in Chapter 2, it says:

> Peer support schemes should be led and designed by children and young people or by parents and carers, with careful professional support to reduce and manage risk both to peer mentors and the young people and families they are involved with.
>
> (DoH and NHS, 2015: 41)

The DfE has also come out in favour of such schemes and, in 2016, launched a Call for Evidence, in which two key questions were asked:

1    What existing approaches are being used that support mental wellbeing?
2    What lessons should we apply from this so that peer support can be developed further?

Overlapping with the Call for Evidence, the DfE commissioned a review of the available models of peer support to improve children's and young people's mental health, although the review eventually expanded to include related topics such as bullying, transitions, wider wellbeing and friendships. The review found that, in addition to different approaches, the terminology varied and included: peer support, peer mentoring, befriending and buddying. The examples were divided into five different models:

- School-based one-to-one support
- School-based group support
- Training-based projects
- Online projects
- Community-based projects

The success of the projects depended less on what type of model was being followed and more on having trained and enthusiastic peer supporters, who had strong communication and interpersonal skills and who themselves were given supervision and support (Coleman et al., 2017).

### Pupil voice

Another way of building confidence and helping young learners to become more resilient is through making sure they feel, and are, involved in the life of the educational setting they are in. As with the need to work in partnership with parents, schools have come a long way in working in partnership with pupils, not in the same way as seeing them as equals in co-production, but in giving pupils every opportunity to feel they are part of the school community and can contribute to its current and future development. A school which has positive policies for behaviour and anti-bullying will help to make it a school which will not only increase pupils' resilience but will be a place they will look back on with many happy memories.

### Factors within the community

The risk factors in a community may be associated with areas of socio-economic disadvantage, homelessness, discrimination and exploitation, or other overwhelming events that affect a neighbourhood. The protective factors include good housing and a good standard of living, having an extended support network of neighbours and friends, access to a broad range of sport and leisure facilities, and a chance to take on social roles within the local community. Now that schools are no longer closed communities sufficient unto themselves but outward-facing institutions, no matter how much or little the local area has to offer, schools may like to consider how to help their students make the most of their surroundings and feel connected to a wider community beyond that of their school or college. This may be by taking up a hobby, joining a sports club or volunteering. Any of these can be a source of satisfaction which can boost confidence and self-esteem. It also involves interacting with the real world rather than communicating via social media.

It is reassuring for those working in schools and colleges to know that, although there are many factors not under their control, schools and other educational settings can make a real difference to the wellbeing of those they teach. As a prerequisite, schools must also be concerned with the wellbeing of their staff. Rather like the warning when flying, that it is no good rushing to help someone before putting on your own oxygen mask first, staff who have low wellbeing will not be in a good place to bolster the wellbeing of their students. (There is more in Chapter 6 about staff wellbeing.) It has been mentioned before that the way schools are made to operate is not always conducive to the wellbeing of staff or of pupils. On one hand, special schools and AP may have more leeway, but, on the other hand, their populations are likely to need significantly more support to give them a sense of emotional wellbeing.

In Northern Ireland, Education Other Than at School (EOTAS) includes all forms of education taking place outside the formal school environment, in a similar way to AP in England. Children with the most serious social, emotional, behavioural, medical or other problems are educated in EOTAS and some will have been excluded from their mainstream schools. Loughshore Education Resource Centre in Belfast (which was also mentioned in the opening chapter) is an EOTAS centre. Its principal, Geri Cameron, points out the different curriculum that some students need, and that one of the pressures on schools, and a barrier to learning for some, is the government being hung up on pupils achieving five GCSEs:

> At Loughshore, we have set up a car valeting business, we have vocational training and our pupils are now chefs across the city, in restaurants and on cruise ships. We have tailored our training to the skills gaps. Our pupils are in jobs that are front of house in the hospitality industry and are highly skilled. They also work in the tech industry, for example with mobile phone companies. We need to acknowledge the potential of people in ways other than test results, the type of school they go to and having five GCSEs.

A fixation on children conforming to the same rigid curriculum, being forced to meet inappropriate qualifications and acting as if everyone is heading off to university, is at odds with building the emotional wellbeing of every young learner, whether they are under pressure because they are expected to do well or fighting against the odds to succeed.

## Children and young people at greater risk

It is apparent that some young people, whether through their genetic inheritance, their family circumstances or their experiences, are less resilient than others and therefore more likely to succumb to developing mental health problems. Sometimes 'vulnerable groups' are talked about, which is a phrase some prefer to avoid because it is over-used and applies to many different groupings, for example, being used interchangeably with 'disadvantaged groups'. However, it is clear that some young people are more easily affected by events that others take in stride. The word 'vulnerability' comes from the Latin word for 'wound', so we could say that those who are vulnerable to developing mental health difficulties include those who have been wounded by life's events, whether as a result of their genetic make-up or from being overwhelmed by negative life experiences.

'Time for Change', a social movement launched in 2007 with the help of funding from the DHSC, Comic Relief and the Big Lottery Fund, was established to change the way people think and act about mental health problems. It points out that mental health issues can affect anyone and that, statistically, one in four of us will experience a mental health problem in any given year and that no one should have to fear being treated differently because of it, pointing out that it is hard enough without having to face the judgement, shame and isolation that often surrounds mental health issues. On its website, there is this quote:

> 28% of young people with mental health problems told us that negative reactions from others had made them want to give up on life.

While many children will go out of their way to support those who need it, a minority may pick on those they see as different in some way. In the DfE document mentioned earlier about peer support, the DfE lists what it calls 'vulnerable groups' as follows:

A child might be described as vulnerable if he or she:

- is disabled and has specific additional needs or has special educational needs
- has returned home to their family from care, or is a young carer
- is showing signs of engaging in anti-social or criminal behaviour
- is in a family circumstance presenting challenges for the child, such as substance abuse, adult mental health problems and domestic violence
- is showing early signs of abuse and/or neglect.

(2016: 11)

It is also useful to recall the close link between physical and mental health and the not-insignificant number of children whose schooling is part of the hospital education service, which will be discussed shortly. The following paragraphs cover some of the groups listed by the DfE as being vulnerable.

### Disadvantaged pupils

There are many schools working with pupils who come from disadvantaged backgrounds that go out of their way to make up for their pupils' lack of opportunities by giving them a rich and varied curriculum. Although not all such schools are in cities, the case study that follows is about Claremont Primary School in Manchester.

### Case study of Claremont Primary School

The school is part of 'Heart of Manchester', a partnership of six schools in central Manchester, which are characterised by many of the pupils being entitled to free school meals (FSM), having English as an additional language (EAL) and presenting high levels of pastoral challenge. One of the tools the school uses to assess pupils' social and emotional wellbeing is the Boxall Profile, which was described in the first chapter of this book.

The school fully appreciates the benefits of being bilingual, while recognising that pupils whose first language is not English may need some support in becoming fluent. The school has a specialist EAL teacher who leads a team of bilingual and EAL assistants so that these pupils can have both the curriculum and pastoral support they require.

## Case study   Claremont Primary School, Manchester

The school has the capacity for 700 pupils, many of whom come from backgrounds that make them more prone to developing mental health issues, such as being in temporary housing or seeking asylum. The school works with a number of outside agencies that support children and their families, including CAMHS, the Educational Psychology Service (EPS) and the police.

Staff are used to observing children closely, so they are in a position to notice any changes in behaviour that might indicate the need for additional support. After using the Boxall Profile questionnaire (https://new.boxallprofile.org/) if it is felt that a pupil might have social, emotional or behavioural needs, class teachers can draw on a range of support, such as counselling, art therapy, play therapy or horticultural therapy. Some of these are provided by Place2Be, the children's mental health charity which operates within the school. In addition, pupils are able to self-refer themselves to the counselling service. This takes place during breaks and lunchtimes so pupils do not miss lessons.

The commitment of the SLT is seen as paramount and the school has invested heavily in staff being trained to identify mental health concerns. This has helped to develop their understanding of pupils who have social, emotional and mental health issues (SEMH). The school's expectations of behaviour can be summed up as follows:

Look after yourself
Look after each other
Look after the school

The head teacher, Anne Conboy, says:

> Without an experience of happiness and a sense of wellbeing in our lives, it is difficult to thrive and to become the best we can be. At Claremont Primary we promote a culture where the safety and wellbeing of our children is a collective responsibility.

### Children with medical needs

Every LA has a legal responsibility to provide education for children whose illness prevents them from attending school. Hospital education covers the education of children and young people who are unable to attend school due to physical and/or mental health difficulties. It includes:

- A school within a hospital
- A medical pupil referral unit (PRU) or AP academy
- CAMHS inpatient units
- Outreach services such as home tuition

Hospital education is different from Elective Home Education, where parents have made a choice to home educate, although, in both cases, children may be educated at home. In 2017 the National Association for Hospital Education (NAHE) was formed to support professionals working in hospital education.

### Case study of Leicester Children's Hospital School

The case study that follows is about a children's hospital school in Leicester, which is a member of the Ash Field Teaching School Alliance.

## Case study   Leicester Children's Hospital School

The Leicester Children's Hospital School provides education for pupils who are too ill to attend their local school. Some of the education is part-time and the majority of pupils are dual-registered with their home school.

One school site is at the Leicester Royal Infirmary Hospital, where education is provided for primary and secondary pupils who are patients on the children's wards.

Willow Bank School is the school's second site in Leicester. This is for secondary-aged pupils who need longer-term provision and who are unable to attend school due to their mental or physical health. It is a fully functioning secondary school with spaces for a wide range of subjects, including art and drama, science, food and sports.

The third site is the CAMHS Unit at Glenfield Hospital which provides education for inpatients aged 13 to 18 years. This is delivered alongside the support they receive for their significant mental health needs. The learning is personalised and geared towards supporting students in regaining their confidence and self-belief during a difficult time in their lives.

The school's Outreach Team provides home tuition for pupils who are unable to attend the school because of their medical needs and ill health. Teaching is one-to-one and linked to the curriculum in the pupil's home school so that they are prepared for a return when that becomes possible.

The school is a partner in the Learning at Home and in the Hospital (LeHo) European project, which has produced materials in Arabic, Catalan, English, Flemish, French, German, Italian and Spanish.

In addition to its other work, the school offers a range of CPD courses, as well as covering schools' mental health policies, designing a medical needs policy and what 'reasonable adjustments' might look like, and other topics that may be difficult to find elsewhere. Recently, these have included:

- An introduction to acquired brain injury (ABI)
- Managing self-harm in young people
- Managing young people with attachment difficulties
- Supporting children with gender identity
- Supporting the education of young people with cancer
- Understanding and managing anxiety in school
- Understanding borderline personality disorder
- Understanding eating disorders
- Dialectical behaviour therapy (DBT) training

DBT is a type of cognitive-behaviour therapy (CBT). However, whereas CBT tries to change negative ways of thinking and behaving, DBT is more concerned with helping to regulate intense emotions and improve relationships. The school uses the NHS 'Five ways to wellbeing' mentioned earlier in this book (NHS, 2008/2020). Pupils' spiritual, moral, social and cultural (SMSC) development is promoted through the curriculum and in day-to-day interactions. (Further information on how schools promote SMSC development is covered in the next chapter.)

### Looked-after children (LAC)/young carers

Others vulnerable to developing mental health issues are those who are LAC; have moved from foster care to being adopted; and young carers, who often have so much weight on their young shoulders that unless the school is both aware and supportive, they can find coping with everything to be too much. These young people are mentioned in the next case study.

## Bullies and the bullied

Bullying is generally understood as behaviour by an individual or group, repeated over time, that is intended to hurt another individual or group either physically or emotionally. Bullying can take many forms such as teasing, name-calling, jostling, punching or physical assault, or isolating/not speaking to someone.

All state-funded schools are required to have behaviour policies which include measures to prevent bullying and how to deal with it when it occurs. Bullying behaviour often emerges in childhood, and the consequences for victims can last a lifetime and have a deleterious effect on their physical and mental wellbeing.

In addition to the responsibility being with the bully, those who support the behaviour as active, or even passive, bystanders are also culpable. And whilst society at large engages in bullying and aggressive behaviour, children and young people will copy those behaviours. In societies where violence towards others is not rewarded, bullying is rarely a problem. For the bully, it is often the sense of power over others that is what they are seeking. If others join in so that they are on the winning side, a bully's self-esteem may get a boost and they will feel rewarded. As previously stated, while many children will go out of their way to befriend children who stand out as being different in some way, there are others who seem drawn to make fun of those who they see as not like them. Part of wanting to bully seems to stem from an imbalance of power, where the bully puts others down in order to elevate themselves.

Dr Emily Lovegrove, who is sometimes referred to as the Bullying Doctor, not because she is a bully – far from it – but because she has spent many years studying bullying behaviour, looks at it from a rather different angle. She has developed 'The Lovegrove Approach', where the starting point is that as the bully is unlikely to change if they are gaining power and self-esteem from bullying, the way to tackle the problem is by helping the victim to change instead. So Lovegrove aims to give them the strategies to cope and make themselves less of a target (https://thebullyingdoctor.com).

This is a question of reigning in the self-esteem of the bully, by helping the 'victim' to appear confident, so they do not send out the wrong visual cues. They need to change the negative feelings about themselves into a more positive outlook. Children who feel bad about themselves give out subtle visual clues to others about how they can be treated and become easy targets. As part of giving former victims the right demeanour, Lovegrove says that the most important thing you wear is your expression! In addition to her books and website, another useful source of support is The National Bullying Helpline (www.nationalbullyinghelpline.co.uk/ and www.anti-bullyingalliance.org.uk). Their advice echoes that of Emily Lovegrove and includes:

> You're the one who's upset so it's going to have to be you who changes rather than the bully. Not easy but you can do it.
>
> If you get bullied it's not because you deserve it somehow.
>
> Don't feel isolated! Everyone gets bullied. But there are tricks for dealing with it – and all you need to do is learn them.
>
> The people who cope with bullying best score highly on tests for social resilience and you can learn that.

### Cyberbullying

A newer phenomenon has been the rise in cyberbullying, where the internet and digital technologies are used to upset or humiliate another person. Anti-bullying policies need to include guidance on cyberbullying and many of them already do. Young people need to be educated on how to use social networks safely, so they can enjoy the benefits without finding themselves in difficult situations. The term 'digital literacy' is now being used as a way of stressing the importance of young people being able to understand and use technology and become aware of the pitfalls as well as the benefits.

Another source of information is the 'Anti-Bullying Alliance', which, in 2002, was established by the National Society for the Prevention of Cruelty to Children (NSPCC) and the National Children's Bureau (NCB), and is hosted by the NCB. Each year the Anti-Bullying Alliance coordinates 'Anti-Bullying Week' in schools across England. More recently, an award for school staff who go beyond the call of duty to support children with issues such as bullying, family life, relationships and health, has been introduced. Its unique feature is that *pupils* nominate the member of school staff they think should win the award and the winners are chosen by a panel of young people.

The report of an inquiry established by The Children's Society and Young-Minds into the impact of cyberbullying on young people's mental health, declared that:

> The direct impact of cyberbullying on children's mental health and well-being is yet to be extensively examined. The inquiry heard evidence to

suggest that the 'disinhibition' effect and the lack of respite that children experience may mean that online bullying can have at least as much of an impact on mental health as it does offline – if not more.

(2018: 40)

The report goes on to quote Liam Hackett, Chief Executive of the anti-bullying charity 'Ditch the Label', who pointed out that:

Thirty years ago, home was a safe place, but now there is no escape from the bullying, which creates constant stress and anxiety which is hard to navigate.

(2018: 40)

In addition to 'Ditch the Label', which is aimed at young people under 25 and is developing an international dimension, another useful resource is 'WISE KIDS', a not-for-profit company, founded in October 2002 to promote safe internet use. The company believes the internet, and digital and mobile services, are transforming the way we live, learn, socialise, do business, access entertainment and more. As a result, it seeks to harness the power of these technologies, while being aware of any negative effects on young people's well-being. There is plenty of information for all those who are interested in young people's online and digital media use, digital literacy, digital citizenship, online rights and safety.

## Restorative Practice

One of the ways that is used for resolving bullying and other disputes is through 'Restorative Justice' or 'Restorative Practice' as it is often called in schools. A review of bullying by the Education Policy Unit (EPU), found that:

Restorative justice programmes have been effective in New Zealand and Australia, reducing truancy and exclusions as well as improving relationships with staff and parents. Additionally, data from UK schools shows that rates of success in stopping bullying were highest in schools with consistently restorative approaches (79 per cent) and lower in schools that were inconsistently restorative (64 per cent) or not restorative at all (58 per cent).

(2018: 11)

---

### Information point    Restorative Practice

A restorative approach places the emphasis on repairing the harm that has been done. This is accomplished through giving all those involved the chance to think about what happened and to describe the incident from their point of view.

Typically, a facilitator asks five set questions, although these may vary slightly depending on the ages of those involved and the role each of them played. The questions cover:

- What do you think happened?
- What were you thinking?
- How are you feeling now?
- Who do you think has been affected?
- What needs to happen to put things right?

This process does not start from apportioning blame, but seeks to repair relationships by giving all those concerned a way of reflecting on their actions and to take responsibility for them. A solution-focused approach is used to agree what needs to happen going forward. This does not need to be apologizing or 'making up', although that can often be a by-product of the process.

This approach is sometimes contrasted with 'Zero Tolerance Policies', where the focus is on whether a rule has been broken rather than on the feelings of the victim.

### Case study of Baycroft School

A school that uses Restorative Practice is Baycroft School in Hampshire, where behaviour and welfare are high on the school's agenda. There is a focus on the STEAM subjects: science, technology, engineering, arts and mathematics to reflect the local context, destination industries and to help prepare pupils for life beyond school. These subjects also help to develop the skills of observation; questioning; problem-solving; abstract thinking and, above all, curiosity about the world.

## Case study   Baycroft School, Fareham

Baycroft is a day community special school for around 180 secondary-aged students who experience learning difficulties; physical, sensory and language challenges; and autism.

The curriculum is focused on the qualities and attributes which the whole community has agreed are keys to lifelong success and happiness. These are:

- Creativity
- Curiosity
- Independence

- Resilience
- Self-regulation

The school is divided into faculties, with one faculty being named the Faculty of Wellbeing. It is responsible for physical education (PE); religious education (RE); PSHE; citizenship; spiritual, moral, social and cultural development (SMSC); and philosophy for children (p4c).

One of the assistant heads, who is a trained social worker, leads on safeguarding, children in need (CiN), pastoral development, therapeutic interventions and inter-agency liaison, working alongside many other staff who are involved in these aspects of the school's work.

Baycroft School worked very closely with the DfE, Hampshire County Council and the PSHE Association as 'early adopters' of the new, statutory relationships and sex education (RSE) content in order to tailor it to the needs of the students.

(There is more about RSE in the next chapter.)

In a conversation with Marijke Miles, the head teacher at Baycroft School, she elaborates on some of these points, including p4c.

## Information point   Philosophy for children (p4c)

The word 'philosophy' comes from the Ancient Greek word 'philosophia' which means 'love of wisdom'.

Philosophy for Children (p4c) and variations of it, has been around for over 40 years in as many as 60 different countries.

The underlying principle is for children and young people to experience rational and reasoned dialogue about things that matter to them and to their teachers.

All participants work together in a 'community of enquiry'. The aim for each child is not to win an argument but to learn how to become clearer, more accurate, less self-contradictory, and more aware of other arguments and values before reaching a conclusion.

### In conversation with Marijke Miles, Head Teacher, Baycroft School

**Q. How did you manage to appoint an assistant head who is a social worker in your previous school and present school?**

A. In both schools where I have been a head teacher, the social worker is a key member of the SLT. In Baycroft, I think it's important that they are embedded in that team. Our social worker has helped to create a school where there is an inherent supervision culture, where staff understand co-construction and are used to working together to problem solve. This means being supported rather than simply passing on a problem. He is currently a .6 assistant head and safeguarding lead and he is developing a Pastoral and Safeguarding service that is based in the school.

The schools are used by the University of Portsmouth and the University of Winchester for extended placements as part of social work degrees for trainee social workers.

**Q. How does the role fit in with others on the staff who have some of the same responsibilities?**

A. Social workers are used to working independently, so when my assistant head started, I asked him to look at safeguarding throughout the school. This meant that he learnt more about how the school staff work as a team, and he taught us how to shift attitudes. Having moved from a different type of special school, I didn't know, for instance, how to recognise the signs of abuse in a pupil with SLD. I got him to system check everything we do for every child and I was amazed by what he discovered. Now he's done that, he can supervise the other assistant heads with their safeguarding responsibilities. He is also the outward-facing part of the school's work in this respect. He also works with our head of therapy to oversee our internal referral system and cycles of interventions, which includes checking their effectiveness and evaluating the outcomes.

**Q. Has the Mental Health Green Paper and the Trailblazer Programme made any difference to how you work? Do you, for example, have a Mental Health Lead?**

A. Although part of the LA is involved in the Trailblazer Programme and the secondary school on the same site falls into the right area (Gosport), we are a roundabout away! However, we've always had a good working relationship with CAMHS, so it's less important for us than some other schools to be connected in this way. There is a mental health lead as part of the faculty model. The Pastoral, Safeguarding and Provision (PSP) Team help to achieve a whole-school culture.

I'm not happy with having firm boundaries between roles, or pastoral work, for example, being solely in the hands of ancillary staff. We don't work in silos. The school is divided into faculties for subjects, as well as having tutor groups. The same supervising team for each key stage ensure that Section F of the EHC plan is monitored closely. This is because, in our view, wellbeing needs cannot be fully met if learning needs are not fully met.

**Q. Have you changed the way you deliver PSHE to accommodate the RSE curriculum?**

A. One of the resources we use is *1decision*, as it provides a framework for mapping what is covered and helps our own internal planning. We also use Hampshire's scheme, the PSHE Association's and many other resources.

We were an early adopter of the new RSE curriculum and Philosophy for Children (p4c) is our starting point for mental health as it provides a very clear explanation of spirituality. Staff are experts in their age group by staying put while children move through. Therefore they become experts in the curriculum, because our tutors teach their own age groups what we call Personal Development and Philosophy (PSHE/RSE/p4c). Although age-based, the content evolves depending on the needs of each group. All the pupils in the school are verbal and what they need to be able to do is to generalise their learning across subjects and scenarios.

Q.  **How do you cover citizenship and SMSC?**

A.  Citizenship is partly tied to our Reward System, with the head being seen as lead citizen in the school. Every week, there's a raffle to take over the Head's role and I sit as a pupil in the classroom. Oracy from p4c and self-advocacy are very much part of this. Under Dis/Ability, pupils discuss what their diagnosis means and how it gives them strong points as well as problems. Sometimes they want to explain to their peers what they know about it and how it affects them.

There are large numbers of Looked-After Children (LAC)/Children in Care (CiC) in school. We also run a group for Young Carers who may be the oldest in a family with needs and will be helping the younger ones. For them, we use the Circle of Friends model, so they can each invite one other person who isn't a carer which helps to overcome any stigma. We link with outside agencies to ensure families are getting the support they need.

Q.  **What particular approaches or interventions, such as Restorative Practice, have you found to be effective in your school?**

A.  I was lucky to study with Henry Kiernan, who is one of the most experienced trainers in the field and I've taken this approach into several schools. I find that it can take time to get it going, then it bubbles up and becomes an inherent part of practice. It may become less evident because it is embedded in the school's approach. For example, the staff will carry round with them the five questions and all the children know them as well, but increasingly they may use them less rigorously because they know how to adapt them to different situations and the principles will still be there.

Q.  **Are there other aspects of your school's work in relation to the emotional wellbeing of staff, for instance, that you would like to mention?**

A.  Staff's wellbeing should stem from the satisfaction they get from doing the job. The consistent feeling of being trusted, valued and part of a great team is universal and sustainable. Although the job is tough, the fundamental rewards should be the job itself. My part has been to pare everything down that doesn't have a direct impact on the children. Before, there was a very hierarchical structure and a 'need to know' basis to safeguarding. Now the human story wraps round everything and staff need to be able to follow each story to its end, for example for a pupil who has a Child Protection Plan (CPP), because they have become a part of that child's story. We like to know that all our staff can see, feel and talk about the impact of what they do for pupils and know each day has been well spent.

In this conversation, Marijke mentions Circle of Friends, which is an approach designed to help pupils and others who are experiencing difficulties in school due to having a disability, being at a point of personal crisis, or because of their challenging behaviour towards others. It encourages the young person's peers to provide support and engage in problem-solving with them. The approach is not the same as circle time although there are similarities. Solution Circles were mentioned in a previous case study and are seen as a quick way of sorting out a problem through people being prepared to ask for help and then working together on the answer (https://inclusive-solutions.com/circles/circle-of-friends/).

## Exclusions and mental health issues

There are three main reasons pupils are excluded from school because of their behaviour. These are:

- Constant, low-level disruption
- Behaviour that is challenging for staff and sometimes for other pupils as well
- One-off incidents that are so serious that exclusion is seen as the only possible response

In the DfE's non-statutory advice mentioned earlier in this chapter, under a paragraph on exclusions, it says:

> When considering excluding a pupil, schools should consider any contributing factors that are identified after an incident of poor behaviour has occurred, which could include where the pupil has mental health problems.
>
> (2018: 17)

All too often, the pupil's mental health is not considered. And yet it is known that having mental health issues places pupils at risk of being excluded. For those whose mental health was not a problem before they were excluded, the very act of being sent away from school can lead to developing mental health problems. For those who already have mental health issues, whether or not they have been recognised, being excluded is likely to exacerbate them. However, although it is easy to criticise schools for excluding pupils, this can be one of the hardest situations for school leaders to deal with. An aggressive child, for instance, may target other pupils and complaints from parents will come rolling in. So, how do you decide between a pupil whose mental health may suffer from being excluded and the other pupils who are being adversely affected by their behaviour? Similarly, staff who are on the receiving end of violent behaviour may look to the SLT to support them.

Again, from the school's point of view, they may feel they have tried everything before being driven to exclude the child and there is nothing else they can do. The reduction in Behaviour Support Teams, autism specialists and other outside agencies, have suffered from a series of cuts made by LAs trying to balance the books. EPs, who can be such a valuable source of advice, are too thin on the ground and, when they are in schools, are likely to spend so much of their time on statutory work that they have little, if any, time to advise the school more generally.

Some schools, particularly for secondary-aged pupils, will have their own form of internal exclusion, whereby students spend time away from their peers. These go under a variety of names, including isolation booths. One mother of an autistic daughter said on TV (Victoria Derbyshire programme April 2019) that she reckoned her daughter had been put in isolation more than 240 times during her time at a secondary school, which had a devastating effect on her mental health and emotional wellbeing. A website called 'Ban the Booths' has been set up to campaign for their eradication and, in 2020, a national conference organised under the name 'Lose the Booths' was held. This is not to suggest that internal exclusions are never the answer. For some, the short, sharp shock of being removed from class may do the trick. For others, time to reflect away from their peers may bring about a change in behaviour. However, if the same pupils keep appearing in the internal exclusion facility, it suggests that this is not the answer for them.

Another way of solving the difficulty of whether or not to exclude a child has been the 'Managed Move', where, without the need to exclude, two schools agree to give the pupil a chance of having a new start. One of the benefits of groups of schools working closely together means that these agreements are more easily arranged and, for some pupils, they will work. However, for those whose behaviour stems from an underlying cause that has never been brought to the surface, the same thing may happen in the school they have moved to.

It is known that boys are twice as likely to be excluded as girls. When boys experience stressful situations, they tend to externalise their distress, for instance through violence or being physically or verbally disruptive, while girls are more likely to internalise their anxieties, which can result in their developing emotional difficulties at some stage.

Trying to fathom the cause of a student's behaviour by seeing it as a form of communication should be the starting point when they are at risk of being excluded, and every effort should be made to find out why their behaviour is problematic to the school and to their peers. If this results in the pupil still being removed, it needs to be to somewhere more suited to their needs. This is not a criticism of the school, which should not be expected to cope with every child seeking admission, but to ensure that children are at a school that can cope with them and, as importantly, the child can cope with the school.

### Alternative provision (AP)

Most excluded pupils, or those at risk of exclusion, will move on to some form of AP. Although there are many types of AP, the most common are PRUs and AP academies. Since 2014, as part of its drive to increase the number of academies, including free schools, the DfE has encouraged PRUs to become AP Academies and many have done so.

#### Case study of the Wave Multi Academy Trust

The Wave Multi Academy Trust (MAT) delivers education to pupils across Devon and Cornwall who are designated 'disengaged' and have been excluded, are at risk of exclusion, attend on an intervention basis, or because of a medical need. The The chief executive, Robert Gasson, says it is most effective when the provision is used as an early intervention strategy to help pupils re-engage with learning. Pupils are admitted through a Pupil Placement Panel or a Medical Referral Panel drawn from local schools. The aim is for maximum stays to be for three or four terms. However, pupils arriving at KS4 are unlikely to return to their schools, so the focus is on preparation for integration into the world of work or FE.

The Wave MAT is made up of eleven regional academies and medical academies which go across Devon and Cornwall. Recently, the Wave MAT became the sponsor of a Special Free School in Devon, which will provide specialist provision for students with social communication and interaction needs, including those on the autism spectrum.

As there is insufficient space to include all the Wave Academies in the following case study, three have been selected to give an idea of how they have a common purpose as part of the same MAT, but each has developed according to its location and intake. The medical AP academies have not been included, as some of their work is similar to that of the Children's Hospital School mentioned earlier in this chapter.

### Case study   Wave MAT provision in Devon and Cornwall

Caradon Academy is situated in Liskeard, SE Cornwall, a region that includes some of the most socially and economically deprived rural areas in the county. The school provides for 40 pupils across Key Stages 1–4. Learning Mentors promote the pupils' self-regulation by improving their social, emotional and behavioural skills, as well as developing resilience for learning. A Family Support Manager ensures that there is clear communication and support for families from admission to reintegration.

Nine Maidens Academy supports students from the Camborne, Redruth area and the Lizard Peninsula. The school is split into a primary and secondary department. In the primary classes, a Trauma informed approach is used to assess emotional and developmental needs and ensure that these needs can be met so that every child is ready to learn, can enjoy being at school and is able to access the wide range of learning opportunities that the school provides. A variety of tried-and-tested resources are used to support emotional development, including those with a focus on anger management, emotional literacy and social skills. In the secondary provision, the department includes a KS3 Nurture provision for pupils who follow a similar curriculum, but it is delivered by the Nurture teacher instead of moving around to different teachers and takes place mainly in the Nurture classroom. All students have opportunities to participate in a range of outdoor activities to develop teambuilding and communication skills.

The Shoreline Academy is on two sites in North Devon; early years and primary pupils are based in Bideford and secondary pupils in Barnstaple. Primary pupils learn through creative and sensory activities, games, songs, stories and YouTube videos. They study neuroscience, emotions and feelings; friendship, internet safety, road safety and stranger danger; the importance of telling the truth; and the factors for keeping a healthy mind and body. They learn strategies for dealing with powerful feelings and emotions and who they can talk to for help and support. At KS3, students follow cross-curricular, project-based learning to link lessons and subjects together. At KS4, as well as GCSEs and BTECs, students can take courses in home cooking skills, motor vehicle studies, and food hygiene, as well as British Canoeing Awards, St John Ambulance First Aid Awards and the Angling Trust Cast Award.

All the Wave Academies make full use of their locations and Learning Outside the Classroom (LOtC), which is discussed in Chapter 6 of this book, is used to build confidence and self-esteem in young people who may not have had the opportunity to experience outdoor activities such as surfing, canoeing, fishing, orienteering and rock climbing.

## Conclusions

While most pupils will flourish in mainstream classes, a minority may benefit from a short (or long) time in AP to receive the support they need in a smaller, more individualised setting. In addition to providing a fresh start for pupils who have already been excluded, AP has a significant role to play in providing outreach services to support pupils to remain where they are, and also in taking in pupils who are at risk of exclusion rather than waiting until it happens.

The next chapter looks at how mental health and emotional wellbeing are becoming a recognised part of the school curriculum and the importance of helping children and young people to become more resilient is part of these changes. Many schools and colleges are actively promoting the importance of resilience, and it is a step forward for a government to make both physical and mental health a statutory part of the school curriculum.

## References

Blincow, D., Hart, A., and Thomas, H. (2016) *Resilient Therapy: Working with Children and Families*. London: Brunner Routledge.

The Children's Society and YoungMinds (2018) *Safety Net: Cyberbullying's Impact on Young People's Mental Health-Inquiry Report Summary*. Available from https://youngminds.org. uk/media/2190/pcr144a_social_media_cyberbullying_inquiry_summary_report.pdf

Coleman, N., Groom, C., and Sykes, W. (2017) Peer support and children and young people's mental health. *Research Review*. Available from https://assets.publishing.service. gov.uk/government/uploads/system/uploads/attachment_data/file/603107/Children_ and_young_people_s_mental_health_peer_support.pdf

Department for Business, Energy and Industrial Strategy (2019) *Regulation for the Fourth Industrial Revolution*. Available from www.gov.uk/government/publications/regulation-for-the-fourth-industrial-revolution

DfE (2016) *Peer Support of Children and Young People's Mental Health: A Call for Evidence*. Available from https://assets.publishing.service.gov.uk/government/uploads/system/uploads/ attachment_data/file/603742/Peer_support_analysis_of_call_for_evidence_report.pdf

DfE (2018) *Mental Health and Behaviour in Schools: Departmental Advice for School Staff*. Available from https://assets.publishing.service.gov.uk/government/uploads/system/uploads/ attachment_data/file/755135/Mental_health_and_behaviour_in_schools__.pdf

DfE, Chalen, A., Machin, S., Noden, P., and West, A. (2011) *Research Report DfE-RR097 UK Resilience Programme: Final Report*. Available from https://assets.publishing.service.gov. uk/government/uploads/system/uploads/attachment_data/file/182419/DFE-RR097.pdf

DoH, and NHS (2015) *Future on Mind: Promoting, Protecting and Improving Our Children and Young People's Mental Health and Well Being*. Available from https://assets.publishing. service.gov.uk/government/uploads/system/uploads/attachment_data/file/414024/ Childrens_Mental_Health.pdf

Education Policy Unit (2018) *Bullying: A Review of Evidence*. Available from https://epi.org. uk/publications-and-research/bullying-a-review-of-the-evidence/

https://bounceforward.com/healthy-minds-research-project/

https://inclusive-solutions.com/circles/circle-of-friends/

https://new.boxallprofile.org/

https://ppc.sas.upenn.edu/research/resilience-children

https://thebullyingdoctor.com

NHS (2008) *5 Steps to Mental Well Being*. London: NHS (updated in 2020). Available from www.nhs.uk/conditions/stress-anxiety-depression/improve-mental-wellbeing/

Public Health England (2015) *Promoting Children and Young People's Health and Well Being: A Whole School and College Approach.* Available from https://assets.publishing.service.gov. uk/government/uploads/system/uploads/attachment_data/file/414908/Final_EHWB_ draft_20_03_15.pdf

Public Policy Institute for Wales (2016) *Promoting Emotional Health, Well-Being and Resilience in Primary Schools.* Available from http://ppiw.org.uk/files/2016/02/PPIW-Report-Promoting-Emotional-Health-Well-being-and-Resilience-in-Primary-Schools-Final. pdf

Rutter, M. (1987) Psychosocial resilience and protective mechanisms. *American Journal of Orthopsychiatry*, 57, 316–331. Available from https://onlinelibrary.wiley.com/ doi/10.1111/j.1939-0025.1987.tb03541.x

www.anti-bullyingalliance.org.uk

www.goalcast.com/2017/05/11/thomas-edison-quotes-motivate-never-quit/

www.mentallyhealthyschools.org.uk

www.nationalbullyinghelpline.co.uk/

https://solihullapproachparenting.com

# Chapter 5

# Emotional wellbeing in the curriculum

Previous chapters in this book have touched on the need for young people to understand and control their emotions. Interest in emotions goes as far back as the time of Aristotle. The Greek philosopher identified three ways of persuading an audience to agree with an idea being put forward. He described these as *ethos* – making an ethical appeal; *logos* – using logic; and *pathos* – appealing to the emotions. However, what Aristotle was interested in was how to arouse an emotional response in an audience, rather than learning about emotion itself.

Although mental health and emotional wellbeing did not become an official part of the school curriculum in England until September 2020, staff in schools and other educational settings have long recognised a pastoral side to their role. As most secondary schools are on a larger scale than primary schools, and secondary teachers are largely subject specialists who have moving groups of pupils passing through their hands, the pastoral role is more clearly identified. Primary teachers, on the other hand, are largely class based and therefore in a better position to keep a close eye on their pupils and how they are feeling.

## Pastoral care

The term 'pastoral care' referred originally to shepherds caring for their flocks and entered into the educational vocabulary through Michael Marland, an influential head teacher who used it as the title for a book on the subject. Later he became the founding chair of the National Association for Pastoral Care in Education (www.napce.org.uk) which remains an active organisation. Marland saw pastoral care as having six aims:

- To enhance learners' experiences
- To support teaching and learning
- To prepare learners for their next steps
- To ensure that learners benefit from onsite counselling services
- To teach learners to show respect for others
- To maintain an orderly environment

The core of Marland's working definition of pastoral care was looking after the total welfare of the pupil. He saw this as being central to education and not just an additional dimension. Currently, the notion of pastoral care continues alongside a heightened interest in addressing students' mental health and emotional wellbeing. Many schools and colleges were already moving in this direction well before the government's Green Paper on Mental Health gave fresh impetus to the importance of pupils' mental health.

The rest of this chapter focuses on how mental health and emotional wellbeing are becoming more embedded in educational settings, both through the subject areas which form a recognised part of the school curriculum and all the other activities that go on in a school and are part of pupils' wider experiences.

The school curriculum is sometimes divided into:

- The taught curriculum, which is made up of subject areas
- The informal curriculum, which covers other – often voluntary – events, such as lunchtime and after-school clubs, school trips and holiday clubs. These rarely have explicit outcomes or forms of assessment attached to them
- The hidden curriculum, which has no timetabled slot but refers to other learning that happens, such as the values, social and cultural messages that are conveyed both directly and indirectly and might be summed up as creating the ethos of a setting. (This is discussed further in the next chapter.)

## Defining the school curriculum

Since the 1988 Education Act (DfE, 1988) successive governments have kept a tight rein on what schools must teach. The national curriculum (NC), which came in at that time, sets out the subjects that must be taught to pupils between the ages of 5 to 16 (Key Stages 1–4). Both the subjects and what will be taught within them – the programmes of study (PoS) – have undergone many changes since the original concept was found to have far too much content. With the introduction of academies as a new type of state school funded directly from government, how far schools are required to conform to a national curriculum has also varied. In England, academies, like private schools, have more control over what they teach, although English, maths and science remain universal. Putting in details of the NC and the PoS at any given point in time is a risky business. However, the information that follows is given in order to convey a sense of what needs to be covered and how mental health and emotional wellbeing fit in with the rest of a school's curriculum.

### The early years foundation stage (EYFS) (DfE, 2017)

Children start school and formal education earlier in England than elsewhere in the UK, with Wales extending the foundation stage to the start of KS2

(7-year-olds). Many other countries in Europe see the sense in leaving formal education until later. The early years foundation stage (EYFS) is for children up to the age of 5 years, including those who are in preschool provision, nursery and reception classes. Since its latest revision, it has consisted of seven main areas of learning and development:

Three of these are described as 'prime areas':

- Communication and language
- Physical development
- Personal, social and emotional development

The importance of communication and language has been mentioned frequently in this book and a rich language environment provides children from disadvantaged backgrounds, in particular, with a chance to listen, to speak and to become more confident about expressing themselves. Physical development, as well as being active and interactive, includes understanding the importance of physical activity and making healthy choices in relation to food. The section on personal, social and emotional development includes the need to:

- Develop a positive sense of themselves, and others
- Form positive relationships and develop respect for others
- Develop social skills and learn how to manage their feelings
- Understand appropriate behaviour in groups
- Have confidence in their own abilities

All these have a direct bearing on emotional health and wellbeing and may be easier to integrate into young pupils' daily educational experiences before they move on to subject-based teaching. The strong emphasis on developing self-confidence and self-awareness, learning to manage behaviour and feelings and forming fruitful relationships needs to remain an integral part of the curriculum throughout a young person's school career.

The next four strands are seen as being specific areas that strengthen the three prime areas already mentioned. These are:

- Literacy
- Mathematics
- Understanding the world
- Expressive arts and design

While the last two of these areas are valuable for encouraging children to explore their environment and experiment with different materials, an undue emphasis on literacy and mathematical skills serves to widen the gap between those who are ready for formal learning and those who need a play-based, child-centred curriculum for longer.

## The curriculum for KS1–4

The 'basic' school curriculum includes the national curriculum, plus Religious Education (RE), relationships and sex education (RSE) and health education (which is also referred to as the RSHE curriculum). Teaching discrete subjects starts from Year 1, although schools are at liberty to have a more topic-based approach across subjects, provided everything in the PoS for each subject is covered. KS1 & 2 are the primary years; KS3 & 4 are the years in secondary school.

## The national curriculum (NC)

The subjects taught across Key Stages 1–3 are:

> English; maths; science; design & technology (D&T); history; geography; art & design; music; physical education (PE) – including swimming at KS2; computing; ancient & modern foreign language (MFL) at KS2, MFL (KS3); and citizenship (KS3).

At KS4, most pupils work towards GCSE exams and have more choice of subjects. The core subjects of English, maths and science must be taken, as well as the foundation subjects of computing, PE and citizenship. In addition, schools have to offer at least one subject from the areas of: arts, D&T, humanities and MFL.

Personal, social, health and economic (PSHE) education, while not compulsory, is seen as important. The 'health' element is now part of RSHE which must be taught. There is non-statutory guidance and a framework for character education. Although it is not seen as a separate subject, schools must show that the spiritual, moral, social and cultural (SMSC) development of pupils is covered. There is statutory guidance for schools on providing career advice and guidance for pupils between the ages of 8 and 13.

Each country in the UK has a different curriculum. Wales, for example, is planning to introduce a new curriculum in 2022, which seeks to embed health and wellbeing as one of six areas of learning experience:

- Science and technology
- Mathematics and numeracy
- Expressive arts
- Humanities
- Health and wellbeing
- Languages, literacy and communication

(Welsh Government, 2020)

In Scotland, the SHANARRI wellbeing indicators, which enable schools to assess the overall wellbeing of a child, are mentioned in the next chapter, together with a case study of a school in the Shetland Isles (www.gov.scot/policies/girfec/wellbeing-indicators-shanarri/).

## Subjects contributing to mental health and emotional wellbeing

Before introducing the main vehicles for teaching about mental health and emotional wellbeing, namely: RSE, health education and PSHE, it may be useful to dip into other subjects that have overlapping material. In its guidance the DfE states:

> The lead teacher will need to work closely with colleagues in related curriculum areas to ensure Relationships Education, RSE and Health Education programmes complement, and do not duplicate, content covered in national curriculum subjects such as citizenship, science, computing and PE.
>
> (2019d)

The following paragraphs pick out some examples from the PoS for the curriculum subjects mentioned in the quote from the DfE, plus D&T, character education, and SMSC. Two of these are illustrated by case studies of schools, one a primary school and one a secondary school.

### Computing

This was added to England's national curriculum in 2014. Replacing the former ICT curriculum with computing was designed to provide England's schoolchildren, from 5 years of age upwards, with the skills, knowledge and ways of thinking needed to feed into a new generation of computer scientists, technical entrepreneurs and digital citizens. One of the areas the PoS cover in some detail is about teaching pupils how to keep themselves safe online, protect their identity and know where to go for help.

### Science

As part of knowing what living things need to keep them alive and well, by the end of primary school pupils will have been taught about the impact of diet, exercise, drugs and lifestyle on the way their bodies function and how they can be damaged. When pupils start secondary education, science is split into the three sciences; the biology element has the most relevance to wellbeing. This is where the details of a healthy diet are explored in more detail, as well as the consequences of imbalances in the diet, obesity and the effects of recreational drugs (including substance misuse) on behaviour and health.

### Physical education (PE)

Across all four Key Stages (apart from swimming for KS2 pupils), the same requirements apply. These include pupils participating in both individual and team games to learn about teamwork and team building. Under

'Preparation for life and participation', a broad range of activities are followed, in order to develop fitness and promote an active, healthy lifestyle, including through community links and sports clubs.

## Design and technology

Cooking and nutrition is part of the D&T curriculum, where pupils should be taught how to cook and apply the principles of nutrition and healthy eating. In addition to instilling a love of cooking and encouraging creativity, this is seen as a crucial life skill so that pupils know how to feed themselves and others affordably and well, both now and in later life. The PoS include learning where food comes from, how it is grown and about seasonality. Having a healthy diet is seen as an integral part of keeping physically and mentally healthy.

## Citizenship

Citizenship has been compulsory in secondary schools since 2002. The PoS for KS3 & 4, have four aims:

1   Understanding how the UK is governed and how citizens are active participants in its democratic systems of government
2   Knowledge of the law and how laws are shaped by society
3   Developing a commitment to volunteering now and in adult life
4   Being equipped with the skills to manage a money plan for future needs

Although there is non-statutory guidance for citizenship at KS1 & 2, primary schools are not required to follow it. The programme sets out the same headings for both Key Stages:

• Developing confidence and responsibility and making the most of their abilities
• Preparing to play an active role as citizens
• Developing a healthy, safer lifestyle
• Developing good relationships and respecting the differences between people

In 2018, the House of Lords published a highly critical account of the state of citizenship education in English schools (House of Lords, 2018). It called for a statutory entitlement to citizenship education from primary to the end of secondary education, which should be taken into consideration by Ofsted inspectors when deciding if a school should be rated as outstanding.

Some schools have found very effective ways of giving their students every chance to become responsible and active citizenship. They view both PSHE and citizenship as being an effective means of developing social, personal and work-related skills, which lead to being able to play an active role in society.

### Case study of Durham Johnston Comprehensive School

Durham Johnston Comprehensive School has a long history of giving its pupils an in-depth understanding of the attributes needed for personal development and wellbeing. The head teacher, Andrew O'Sullivan, says: 'For the adult members of our community the seven Nolan Principles of public life are crucial. We work to make the young people of our community value such attributes, too'.

---

**Information point   The Seven Principles of Public Life**

The Seven Principles of Public Life outline the ethical standards those working in the public sector are expected to adhere to. They were first set out in 1995 by the Committee of Standards in Public Life, in a report by Lord Nolan. They are often referred to as 'The Nolan Principles'. These are:

- Selflessness
- Integrity
- Objectivity
- Accountability
- Openness
- Honesty
- Leadership

The principles are included in a range of Codes of Conduct across public life (Committee of Standards in Public Life, 2015).

---

The Nolan Principles form part of the school's Behaviour Policy, where they are explained in greater detail.

---

**Case study   Durham Johnston Comprehensive School**

This secondary school in Durham is comprehensive in the sense that pupils come from a wide range of backgrounds but also in the sense that it offers a wide range of curricular and cultural opportunities. Pupils have a broad range of academic opportunities, and the school also provides for their pastoral and wellbeing support, with staff trained to recognise when pupils may need additional support and to be aware of any information in their background that might lead them to be at risk, such as deprivation, having SEND or experiencing recent family trauma. The school uses its knowledge of pupils to tailor the PSHE curriculum and ensure its appropriateness.

The PSHE curriculum is used to enable pupils to identify their own mental health issues and to know how to access relevant support. This includes discussions about how to identify normal stress levels and when to seek help. The overarching aim is to give pupils a sense of perspective as well as the autonomy to manage their own mental health. They can self-refer and the school has part-time counsellors as well as other interventions.

Form groups are central to the pastoral support system and the school works very closely with all its feeder primary partners when planning form classes, with an emphasis on students making new friends. Form tutors stay with the form class for the five years from Year 7 to Year 11. The school also has a Peer Support Group. Part-time counsellors are employed by the school and the Student Support Centre is used for internal exclusion, not just to isolate the student but to combine intensive counselling with catching up on work.

While The Nolan Principles are particularly for adults in the school community, the Behaviour Policy explains that:

> We work to make the young people of our community value such attributes too. . . . If our young people can learn to follow these principles, they are ready to be good citizens, following a national adult paradigm for behaviour.

In 2011, when he was prime minister, David Cameron introduced the idea of a National Citizen Service (NCS) to give teenagers a range of experiences based on service to the community. Brett Wigdortz is its Founder and Honorary President, having moved from setting up 'Teach First', an educational charity working to break the link between low family income and poor educational attainment in England and Wales by training graduates with good degrees to teach in areas of disadvantage. In 2020, Mark Gifford took over as Chief Executive of the National Citizen Service Trust (NCST).

## Information point    National Citizen Service (NCS)

NCS is a voluntary personal and social development programme, funded largely by the UK Government. The programme is open to all teenagers aged 16 to 17 in England and Northern Ireland (NI). It is a four-phase programme run with partner organisations across the country. The Trust works collaboratively to enrich the experience for everyone who takes part, as well as benefitting the wider community in the area.

The NCS brings together young people from different backgrounds and helps them develop greater confidence, self-awareness and responsibility. It encourages personal and social development by working on skills like leadership, teamwork and communication. It runs in the spring, summer and autumn, with participants spending a short time away from home and taking part in a team project of benefit to their local community.

Although there was a hiatus at the height of the pandemic, from 2020 onwards, the NCS plans to work with over 150 partner organisations. These include: local football clubs, charities, councils, not-for-profit organisations and the private sector. These will form a network to deliver the NCS experience. Over 500,000 people have already taken part in an experience which might last for just a few weeks, but the impact is said to last much longer (www.gov.uk/government/news/national-citizen-service).

The final subject mentioned in this section is character education.

### Character education

In February 2019, Damian Hinds, as secretary of state for education, set out five foundations for building character, which were drawn from a much longer list and grouped together:

1  Sport
2  Creativity
3  Performing
4  Volunteering and membership
5  World of work

In 2019, an advisory group was established, which was chaired by Ian Bauckham and included members from the National Association of Head Teachers (NAHT) and the Association of School and College Leaders (ASCL). The group met with teachers, parents, voluntary sector organisations, businesses, and young people. The same year, and following a Call for Evidence (DfE, 2019a) the DfE issued Guidance (DfE, 2019b) based on the group's recommendations. Although the guidance is non-statutory, character education is seen as contributing to SMSC development, which schools have a statutory duty to promote and which will be discussed next.

The guidance proposes six benchmarks which reflect the features of good schools. These are:

A  What kind of school are we?
B  What are our expectations of behaviour towards each other?

C    How well do our curriculum and teaching develop resilience and confidence?
D    How good is our co-curriculum?
E    How well do we promote the value of volunteering and service to others?
F    How do we ensure that all our pupils benefit equally from what we offer?

It is suggested that these benchmarks could be used by schools to identify their current situation and what they might do to take the next steps. In Annex A, there is a long list of organisations that can be drawn on to support this work, including the Association for Character Education, the PSHE Association and the NCS.

In its current School Inspection handbook, when talking about the dimensions of personal development, Ofsted adds its own definition of character which it defines as:

> a set of positive personal traits, dispositions and virtues that informs their motivation and guides their conduct so that they reflect wisely, learn eagerly, behave with integrity and cooperate consistently well with others. This gives pupils the qualities they need to flourish in our society.
>
> (2019: 218)

### Case study of Crosshall Junior School

The next case study is about Crosshall Junior School in St Neots, Cambridgeshire. Among its many other links, the school was an original partner in Whole Education (WE).

---

### Information point   Whole Education (WE)

Whole Education (www.wholeeducation.org) is a national network of over 500 schools and partners who believe that children and young people are entitled to have a fully rounded (or whole) education. It was founded in 2010 to respond to a concern that an undue focus on pushing up exam results has been at the expense of providing the broad education all pupils are entitled to receive. WE developed further through the Royal Society of Arts's 'Charter for 21st Century Education' and conversations with leaders across the field of education.

These conversations led to WE seeking to make learning more relevant and engaging, with pupils and students being able to take ownership of their own learning. Rather than leading to a lowering of standards, this change is seen as a way of narrowing the attainment gap and preparing all young people for their futures.

WE was started by Sir John Dunford, a former general secretary of the Association for School and College Leaders (ASCL) and Lord Knight (formerly known as Jim Knight, when he was a Labour secretary of state for education) is the chair.

In addition to its involvement in WE, Crosshall Junior School has a very evident concern for the wellbeing of its pupils and the school ensures that character education is part of the pupils' experience.

## Case study   Crosshall Junior School, St Neots

Crosshall is a standalone junior academy, where character building, combined with a growth mindset, helps its pupils to become responsible citizens who develop the skills and knowledge to achieve their future dreams. The school's values are summed up by the acronym ARK, which stands for:

- Ambition
- Resilience
- Kindness

The school promotes pupils' self-esteem and emotional wellbeing, helping them to form and maintain worthwhile and satisfying relationships, based on respect for themselves and for others, at home, at school, at work and in the community.

The school has a 'Future Me' programme, which rewards children who, regardless of academic ability, take risks, try something new, participate in social action and build character. In addition, the pupils have an opportunity to meet and ask questions of people from a wide variety of occupations and the school uses these visits to break down gender stereotypes. The programme has led to the school becoming one of the first winners of the DfE's Character Awards, known as the '#IWill Awards' given for building character and resilience. This can be demonstrated by young people who take practical action to make a positive difference through formal or informal activities. These include volunteering, fundraising, campaigning or supporting peers.

An Anti-Bullying Council run by the pupils writes a termly newsletter to parents to keep them informed of the work they are doing. The council has written a children's version of the school's anti-bullying policy. At breaktimes, pupils who feel upset or lonely can sit on a Friendship Bench and members of the Anti-Bullying Council or Peer Mediators will offer help and support.

The head teacher, Anne Eardley, explains:

> Our marking and feedback policy recognises that the children are on a learning journey and our use of 'not yet' encourages students to think through problems. Encountering challenges indicates that a child is learning and it is when a child bounces back from difficulties that confidence, resilience and drive are developed. The deepest learning often comes through adversity and perfectionists have their thinking challenged.

The final part of this section is not about another subject area but about SMSC, which, rather than being a subject, permeates the whole of the curriculum and helps to create the ethos of a school or setting.

## Spiritual, moral, social and cultural development (SMSC)

A duty that schools should encourage pupils' SMSC development was first introduced in the 1988 Education Reform Act (ERA) and referred to again in the Education Act 2002. In 2014, the government issued guidance which included how promoting British values (DfE, 2014) should be part of SMSC. Work in this area also fits in with the UN Convention on the Rights of the Child (UNICEF, 1989). The Ofsted inspection handbook makes it clear that SMSC education is a high priority for inspectors. In reaching a judgement on a school's overall effectiveness, it says:

> Before making a judgement on overall effectiveness, inspectors will always consider the spiritual, moral, social and cultural development of pupils and evaluate the extent to which the school's education provision meets different pupils' needs, including pupils with SEND
>
> (Ofsted, 2019: 168)

Under 'personal development', there is a whole section on SMSC development, at the start of which it reads:

> Inspectors will evaluate the effectiveness of the school's provision for pupils' spiritual, moral, social and cultural education. This is a broad concept that can be seen across the school's activities, but draws together many of the areas covered by the personal development judgement.
>
> (Ofsted, 2019: 219–222)

This is followed by a useful definition of the four terms within SMSC which can be summarised as follows:

## Spiritual development

*   The ability to be reflective about their own beliefs (religious or otherwise) and perspective on life

- The knowledge of, and respect for, different people's faiths, feelings and values
- A sense of enjoyment and fascination in learning about themselves, others and the world around them
- The use of imagination and creativity in their learning and willingness to reflect on their experiences

## Moral development

- The ability to recognise the difference between right and wrong, legal boundaries, and respecting the civil and criminal law of England
- The ability to understand the consequences of their behaviour and actions
- An interest in investigating views about moral and ethical issues and to appreciate the viewpoints of others on these issues

## Social development

- Using a range of social skills to work and socialise with pupils from different religious, ethnic and socio-economic backgrounds
- Participating in a variety of community and social settings, including by volunteering, cooperating well with others and being able to resolve conflicts effectively
- Accepting the fundamental British values of democracy, individual liberty and mutual respect and tolerance of those with different faiths and beliefs so that they can contribute positively to life in modern Britain

## Cultural development

- Understanding the wide range of cultural influences that have shaped their own heritage and that of others, including the range of different cultures in the school and further afield
- Valuing the things we share across cultural, religious, ethnic and socio-economic communities
- Knowing about Britain's democratic parliamentary system and how it continues to shape our history and values
- Responding positively to artistic, musical, sporting and cultural opportunities
- Respecting different faiths and cultural diversity, as shown by their attitudes towards different religious, ethnic and socio-economic groups in the local, national and global communities

In 2017, the SMSC Quality Mark was launched. Since then, schools have utilised the SMSC Self-Review Tool to shape and inform their provision (www.smscqualitymark.org.uk).

## Main subjects for teaching mental health and wellbeing

The three subjects that were added to the school curriculum in 2020 and contribute to pupils' understanding of mental health and emotional wellbeing are:

- Relationships education (primary)
- RSE (secondary)
- Health education

Following a consultation, the DfE published final statutory guidance in June 2019. Although this did not come into force in September 2020, schools were encouraged to adopt it beginning in September 2019; over 1,500 put themselves forward to be early adopter schools. Although the requirements do not apply to sixth-form colleges, 16 to 19 academies or FE colleges, the DfE encourages them to take them on board. Independent schools are not required to follow the health education guidance as PSHE is already a compulsory subject.

In the foreword introducing the guidance, the secretary of state wrote:

> Teaching about mental wellbeing is central to these subjects, especially as a priority for parents is their children's happiness. We know that children and young people are increasingly experiencing challenges, and that young people are at particular risk of feeling lonely. . . . All of this content should support the wider work of schools in helping to foster pupil wellbeing and develop resilience and character that we know are fundamental to pupils being happy, successful and productive members of society.
>
> (DfE, 2019d)

The guidance mentions that many schools already cover much of the content through a wider programme of PSHE education, and this can continue to be the method of delivery if the school wishes to build on what is already established and working well. In Annex B of the guidance, there is a list of useful teaching resources from the NSPCC, Catholic Education, Stonewall, PHE, MindEd, and many others, including materials from the PSHE Association. (Further details of these organisations are given in Chapter 7.)

### Relationships education and RSE

The original intention was that schools would start teaching relationships education in primary schools beginning in September 2020 and secondary schools would teach RSE beginning at the same time. However, in July 2020, the DfE updated its guidance to say that, with the hiatus caused by the pandemic, these subjects would still be compulsory in the 2020/21 school year, but if a school felt it had insufficient time to prepare to teach the subject, it could delay teaching it until the start of the 2021summer term at the latest. At the same time, the DfE suggested that:

Schools should consider prioritising curriculum content on mental health and wellbeing, as knowledge on supporting your own and others' wellbeing will be important as pupils return to schools.

(2020a: 1)

Primary schools are required to have an up-to-date policy for relationships education and secondary schools should have an RSE policy. In the statutory guidance for these subjects, the DfE sets out what these policies should include. In brief, they should:

1   Define the subject, with primary schools explaining any sex education they plan to teach which is beyond that covered by the science curriculum; secondary schools should include information about a parent's right to request their child does not attend these lessons
2   Set out the content: how it will be taught, who will be teaching it, how the subject will be monitored and evaluated, and when the policy will be reviewed

Schools may wish to add details of the schemes of work they use, how the policy is produced and reviewed with the involvement of parents and how the content will be made accessible to all pupils including those with SEND. In addition to parental involvement, policies should show that the views of teachers and of pupils have been taken on board.

### Relationships education (for primary schools)

The emphasis at this stage is on positive, healthy relationships with family, friends and other people. This provides opportunities for children to learn about how friendships can support emotional and mental wellbeing. By the end of KS2, pupils should have studied:

- Families and people who care for me
- Caring friendships
- Respectful friendships
- Online relationships
- Being safe

(Further details are on pages 19–24 of the guidance.)

### Relationships and sex education (RSE)

The guidance explains that secondary schools do not need to teach these as separate subjects but that teaching about relationships and sex education may be integrated into a single programme. This should build on what pupils have covered in their primary schools, including a continued emphasis on cultivating resilience and character building. Sex education is compulsory from age 11 onwards (apart from parents who request that their children be withdrawn from some or all of sex education delivered as part of statutory RSE). By the end of KS4, when some pupils will have completed their secondary education, they should have covered:

- Families
- Respectful relationships including friendships
- Online and media
- Being safe
- Intimate and sexual relationships, including sexual health

(For further details, see pages 25–30 of the guidance, which includes information on what the law says about sex, relationships and young people, as well as broader safeguarding issues).

### Case study of Bentley Wood High School for Girls

This school in London has a comprehensive RSE policy, which begins with this statement:

> The School acknowledges the importance of its pastoral role in the welfare of young people, and through the general ethos of the school, and the implementation of this policy, will seek to create an environment where pupils feel able to seek advice and help.

### Case study    Bentley Wood High School for Girls, Harrow

Bentley Wood is a National Teaching School and part of the Harrow Collegiate Teaching School Alliance. The school focuses on being 'A community who care', with the word CARE standing for:

- Communication
- Achievement
- Respect
- Empathy

In addition to RSE being taught within the PSHE curriculum, it links to the school's wider curriculum by:

- Promoting the spiritual, moral, cultural, mental and physical development of pupils at the school and of society

- Preparing pupils for the opportunities, responsibilities and experiences of later life

In addition to the PSHE co-ordinators' responsibility for the implementation of the RSE curriculum, tutors are seen as having a pivotal role with regard to the pastoral care of their pupils and in creating a positive ethos and an atmosphere of trust, in which pupils feel confident to discuss sensitive issues.

The heads of year work closely with the SLT to keep the RSE/PSHE curriculum under review and improve its quality. All staff help to ensure that RSE has a high profile within the school.

The school recognises the value of working in partnership with parents and draws on the wealth of expertise available in the whole community. In addition to parents, this includes being able to draw on health professionals, social workers, youth workers and members of voluntary organisations as needed.

In discussions with Janice Howkins, she provided further details of how PSHE and, within it, RSE are integrated into the curriculum and the ethos of the school.

### In conversation with Dr Janice Howkins, Head Teacher, Bentley Wood

**Q. Were you an early adopter of the relationships and sex education (RSE) curriculum. Are you introducing it now, or are you taking up the flexibility the DfE has given schools to postpone it until next summer?**

A. Bentley Wood is an early adopter school for RSE. We created a school improvement group to support the changes required. We have been implementing new RSE-focused lessons for two years now.

**Q. Have you needed to make any changes to the PSHE curriculum in order to accommodate the requirements of RSE?**

A. Yes, but not major ones. Our original PSHE curriculum covered much of the RSE curriculum already.

**Q. Is the 'spiral' approach to teaching RSE mirrored in how other subject areas are taught?**

A. RSE is taught in an age appropriate way and therefore it lends itself to a spiral curriculum model. The wider PSHE curriculum overview is based on the PSHE Association Key Stage Outcomes. It is split up into three main themes which are present in all year groups.

**Q. Do the pupils in the Additionally Resourced Mainstream School (ARMS) provision follow the same PSHE/RSE curriculum?**

A. Yes
Q. **Is spiritual, moral, social and cultural (SMSC) education taught as a separate subject area or incorporated into other subjects or activities?**
A. No, it is incorporated into lessons, school values of CARE and high expectations around behaviour for learning.
Q. **Do you see a role for character education as a discrete area of learning?**
A. No. We believe character education is most effectively implemented across all curriculum areas through a range of activities as well as enrichment. That being said we are in process of developing a character development programme to raise the profile across the school and provide evidence of impact.
Q. **Do you have someone carrying out the role of senior mental health lead (SMHL) and, if so, is that the title you use?**
A. Yes. One of the assistant head teachers (AHTs) carries out that role, but they do not have that specific title.
Q. **Your school has an impressive range of enrichment activities. Are ones such as Resilience Leaders for Y7, Mindfulness and Boxercise used as interventions, or is it left to the pupils whether or not they wish to attend?**
A. It is largely student choice whether they attend. However, we try to incentivise their participation. Some students are asked to join certain clubs, such as Resilience Leaders, by invitation.

### Health education

The section on 'Health' in the guidance is headed, 'Physical health and mental wellbeing'. It begins as follows:

> The aim of teaching pupils about physical health and mental wellbeing is to give them the information that they need to make good decisions about their own health and wellbeing. It should enable them to recognise what is normal and what is an issue in themselves and others and, when issues arise, know how to seek support as early as possible from appropriate sources.
>
> Physical health and mental wellbeing are interlinked, and it is important that pupils understand that good physical health contributes to good mental wellbeing, and vice versa.
>
> (DfE, 2019d: 83 & 84)

The guidance states that primary school children should learn that mental wellbeing is a normal part of daily life and why simple self-care – like getting enough sleep and staying active – is important. The secondary content builds on this to ensure that pupils can spot the signs of common mental illnesses in themselves and in others, and that they know how to discuss their emotions accurately and sensitively.

The rest of the paragraphs are set out in a similar way to RE and RSE, with a list of what pupils should have covered by the end of primary and secondary school, although, in this instance, the list is the same for both. The main topics are:

- Mental wellbeing
- Internet and safety harms
- Physical health and fitness
- Healthy eating
- Drugs, alcohol and tobacco
- Health and prevention
- Basic first aid
- Changing adolescent body

In more detail, during the primary phase, pupils should learn:

- That mental wellbeing is a normal part of daily life in the same way as physical health
- That there is a normal range of emotions
- How to recognise and talk about their emotions, and their own and others' feelings
- How to judge their own feelings and behaviour
- The benefits of physical exercise, time outdoors and community participation
- How to use simple self-care techniques, including rest, time with friends and family, and having hobbies and interests
- That isolation and loneliness can affect children and they need to talk about how they feel
- That bullying has a negative and often lasting impact on mental wellbeing
- How to seek support, including from school

At the secondary level, pupils should be taught:

- How to talk about their emotions
- That happiness is linked to being connected to others
- How to recognise the early signs of mental wellbeing concerns
- Common types of mental ill health (e.g. anxiety and depression)
- How to critically evaluate when something they do or are involved in has a positive or negative effect on their own or others' mental health
- The benefits and importance of physical exercise, time outdoors and community participation

To supplement the statutory guidance, the DfE produced a non-statutory train-ing module on teaching mental wellbeing (DfE, 2020c). The module is a use-ful way of getting across some of the themes listed previously. The resource is designed to be used flexibly, so it can be customised for use by different schools. The slides aimed at primary pupils include a reference to the NHS 'Five steps to mental wellbeing'. Towards the end of the module, there is information on where to find support, such as Childline, YoungMinds and Samaritans. (Further details of these organisations are given in Chapter 7.) The final piece of advice is to convey the message that mental wellbeing is on a spectrum (as mentioned previously) and it is not just a case of being binary – either good or bad:

It is real progress that, at last, children's and young people's mental health and emotional wellbeing are being taken seriously by government. Combined with the work of the Mental Health Trailblazers and all the other steps being taken by educational settings and by the health service, this is very positive and even more necessary in the wake of COVID-19. The final part of this section looks at ways in which schools are addressing these requirements alongside existing programmes they have developed for PSHE.

### Personal, social, health and economic (PSHE) education

PSHE is in the odd position of being a non-statutory subject, but the govern-ment expects all schools in England to make provision for it. It provides funding to various bodies, principally the PSHE Association, to support the teaching of PSHE. Nevertheless, despite remaining non-statutory, most educational set-tings have seen it as central to their role. In its guidance on teaching RSHE already referred to, the DfE says:

> We know that many schools will choose to teach the compulsory content within a wider programme of Personal, Social, Health and Economic Edu-cation or similar. Schools are encouraged to continue to do so, if this is right for them, and build on established, high quality programmes.
>
> (DfE, 2019d: 5)

Although the DfE talks of having specific guidance about PSHE (see references at the end of the chapter), this amounts to four paragraphs and a link to the PSHE Association's website, where the information about teaching PSHE is to be found.

## PSHE Association

On its website, the PSHE Association defines the subject as follows:

> PSHE education is a school subject through which pupils develop the knowledge, skills and attributes they need to keep themselves healthy and safe, and prepared for life and work.
>
> (www.pshe-association.org.uk)

The Association's PoS were updated for 2020/01 and cover KS1–5. This means they have been updated to take on board the curriculum subjects introduced in England beginning in September 2020. The materials for all Key Stages are free to download and available as printed copies for members. The next two case studies provide examples of how PSHE is covered in an AP and in a primary school.

## Case study of Leamington LAMP

Leamington LAMP is an AP based in Warwickshire. Timothy Ellis, the strategic director, explains that the school's core values are:

- Offering a student-centred curriculum
- Helping young people to become independent in life and learning
- Helping young people to understand personal health and safety
- Fostering a growth mindset and an excitement around learning
- Allowing creativity to flourish and to promote equality

The centre does not have traditional classrooms; it is more like an art centre or someone's house. Each area is equipped with high-quality resources required for each activity. In addition, there are theatrical props, unusual objects and vintage or homemade musical instruments scattered around. LAMP students are bright, intelligent, sometimes gifted young people who have suffered a trauma in a mainstream school causing extreme anxiety.

### Case study    Leamington LAMP, Warwickshire

LAMP specialises in working with young people with autism, high anxiety or SEMH. Due to their needs, these young people can become overwhelmed and disengaged in their mainstream schools and some will spend time in hospital. All have EHCPs. LAMP offers students the opportunity to get back into education, often following years of isolation confined to the home. A minority of students come on a day release from a mainstream school where there is recognition that an alternative intervention can be beneficial/motivational. The aim is to re-engage young people in education through the arts and redevelop a social life. Some students will make friends for the first time. The arts and general creative thinking are a critical part of helping them reach their academic potential, making education enjoyable and exciting so that they want to become lifelong learners. This is achieved by:

- Allowing students to use their own ideas to inform study
- Instilling independence and a creative approach to problem-solving
- Helping young people understand and achieve personal health and safety
- Creating an environment that is fun to be in and engaging to learn in
- Creating an exciting, engaging curriculum that has value for progression
- Listening to ideas, empowering students by taking them seriously

To make this possible, the staff includes course leaders in: Art and Music Enrichment; Art, Design and Photography; Music Performance and Technology; Japanese Language and Culture; Theatrical Make-Up; Photography and Computer Game Development. Given access to a broad creative curriculum helps with engagement in core subjects such as maths and English.

PSHE at LAMP offers students all the statutory ingredients such as personal development, health and relationships, financial literacy and British values. In addition, a good portion of mentoring work is done around progression. Mentors will take students walking through local woodland, giving them an opportunity to speak freely about anxieties and aspirations. Students have been empowered to open up about, approach and overcome potential life barriers using this approach.

Some topics, such as RSE and drugs and alcohol, are delivered by trained health professionals. When attending LAMP, students are invited to step outside their perceived comfort zones in a supportive environment, empowering them to prepare for independent living, FE and the world of work.

The is no staff room at LAMP. Staff and students share an open-plan lounge/kitchen and everyone is known by their first name. Students wear what they are comfortable in and staff are in smart casual attire. Breaks and lunchtimes are always a time for conversation, debating and board games with no obvious hierarchy. There is a code of conduct and behaviour contract but these are rarely broken.

In addition to the standard range of policies, LAMP has a School Dog Policy. This explains that children and young people can benefit both educationally and emotionally from having a dog around. Ripley is a female apricot cockapoo chosen for its very mild temperament, hypoallergenic qualities and non-moulting coat. Students can increase their understanding of responsibility and develop empathy and nurturing skills through contact with a dog. Ripley finds the most exciting part of the day is greeting everyone when they arrive at 9AM. She will also spend some of the day briefly visiting lessons.

The pupils who arrive at LAMP are not without ability; many will have been through the mental health system and labelled 'high needs'. LAMP demonstrates that 'high needs' can transition to 'high achiever'. For example, in 2020 a student won a three-year scholarship to study music at the University of Brighton. But because of their level of anxiety or inability to fit in with the expectations and curriculum offered in their previous schools, they needed a different experience and environment to succeed. A poem written by one of the students appears at the end of Chapter 7.

### Case study of Queen's Park Primary School

Queen's Park Primary School is in the London Borough of Westminster. The school has developed an approach that puts mental health and wellbeing at the heart of the curriculum. Both the executive head teacher, Ben Commins, and the head of school, Lyndsy Killip, are MHFA instructors and have been able to train all the staff.

The PSHE curriculum is described as being integral to the school's vision and ethos and is woven into all areas of the curriculum. It itemises the following ten ways to wellbeing:

- Happiness
- Gratitude
- Mindfulness
- Perception
- Perseverance
- Resilience
- Acceptance
- Respect
- Kindness
- Risk taking

The PSHE curriculum is based on the three core themes of mental health, physical health and relationships education. Children from reception class upwards complete the daily mile, which is aimed at encouraging fitness in a social activity.

### Case study   Queen's Park Primary School, Westminster

The PSHE curriculum includes the following elements:

The Zones of Regulation is used as a means of helping children to gain impulse control (self-regulation). Emotions are seen in terms of four colours.

The Blue Zone is for low mood or boredom, while the other three colours follow the traffic light system, with Green for a calm but alert state, Yellow for feeling anxious or frustrated and Red for intense emotions such as anger or terror.

This is complemented by the use of Mind Up, a programme created by the Goldie Hawn Foundation, which aims to help children understand the neuroscience behind emotions. The lessons are designed to foster social and emotional awareness, enhance psychological well-being and promote academic success.

Protective Behaviours is a safety awareness and resilience framework, which helps children to recognise when they feel stressed or unsafe. Through confidence building and an empowering approach, children learn about having adventures and taking risks, while developing a shared language to understand practical ways of keeping themselves safe.

Using elements of these three resources, pupils are given a more complete understanding of themselves, as well as equipping them with tools to explore the three themes of mental health, physical health and relationships education. In addition, looking at how the brain works helps them to understand their own and other people's emotions.

(In Chapter 7, there is information about where to find out more about these approaches.)

In addition to these approaches, the school offers a wide range of targeted interventions to support pupils' emotional wellbeing. These include:

- Bereavement and Emotional Literacy Group
- Resilience Group
- Friendship Group
- Lego and Robotics Group

The wellbeing of parents and all members of the school community is seen as important. To this end, the school has an 'open door' policy where parents are encouraged to talk about any concerns. The school says:

> We strive for our pupils to recognise their individual talents and potential and hope when they leave school that they will be judged not only by their performance during tests but also by the quality of their character.

The final case study in this chapter is about a secondary school which has worked hard over many years to identify and address mental health needs and to raise the emotional wellbeing of its students.

*Case study of Henry Cort Community College*

The college's ASPIRE ethos is summed up in six key values:

- *Achievement*
- *Support*
- *Perseverance*
- *Individuality*
- *Respect*
- *Excellence*

The college recognises that behavioural problems can stem from a student's social and emotional needs or mental health issues and that investing in developing trusting and consistent relationships with students is fundamental. The college uses a vertical tutoring system, whereby tutor groups are made up of small, mixed age groups of students from different years. As far as possible, students stay with the same tutor group and head of house throughout their five years.

The ethos of the college is promoted through a broad set of common values and purposes which underpin the curriculum. The college's commitment to ensuring these happen in practice is shown by its 'Drop Down Wednesday', which incorporates elements of SMSC, citizenship, RSE and PSHE one morning each week. The following case study concentrates on this venture and gives the flavour of what is covered under each of the six strands.

## Case study   Henry Cort Community College, Fareham, Hants

One morning every week, Drop Down Wednesdays enables SMSC, citizenship, and personal development learning to be delivered across the school by specialist teams of staff who are responsible for the resourcing and delivery of one of the six strands. The following description gives an idea of the content covered:

*Relationships and sex education (RSE)* Choices, contraception and conception; healthy relationships; parenting, marriage and living together

*Enterprise and finance* Ethical shopping, running a business, spending and saving, consumer rights and responsibilities.

*Respect* Cyber safety, stranger danger; bullying; drugs and alcohol; stereotypes and diversity; control and freedom of the press.

*Health and wellbeing* Healthy and active lifestyles, body image, preparing for adult life, future options, health and safety awareness

*Democracy* Elections, political parties, the role of local councils, diversity in the UK, crime and punishment, anti-social behaviour, human rights.
*Growth mindsets* How to think with a growth mindset; dealing with stress, anxiety and depression; exam preparation; setting goals

The lessons are age appropriate and can build on what has been covered in previous years, as the same staff will be teaching the content.

These lessons contribute to a healthy lifestyle, which is promoted throughout the curriculum.

The college provides help, support and opportunities that enable all members of the college community to develop resilience and perseverance, allowing them to overcome the barriers and setbacks in everyday life. Another example of this is the 'Drop In' sessions available to all young carers, which take place every Monday at lunchtime. These sessions are run by the young carers lead at the school and supported by the Gosport and Fareham Young Carers branch of KIDS (the national charity providing support to children, young people and their families). Young carers can bring a friend and spend time chatting, playing board games or completing homework, as well as eating their lunch. There is a young carers message box in the foyer where messages or comments can be left. The college has gained a Young Carers Award in recognition for good practice in meeting the needs of this vulnerable pupil group.

## Conclusions

This chapter has concentrated on how changes to the curriculum have encouraged a greater emphasis on mental health and wellbeing and how to incorporate new subjects into both statutory and non-statutory curriculum areas. The next chapter moves on to consider how to ensure that the ethos and environment of an educational establishment can contribute to the mental health and emotional wellbeing of all who work and learn within it.

## References

Committee of Standards in Public Life (2015) *The Principles of Public Life (Nolan Principles)*. Available from www.gov.uk/government/publications/the-7-principles-of-public-life
DfE (1988) *Education Reform Act*. Available from www.legislation.gov.uk/ukpga/1988/40/pdfs/ukpga_19880040_en.pdf
DfE (2014) *Guidance on Promoting British Values*. Available from www.gov.uk/government/news/guidance-on-promoting-british-values-in-schools-published

DfE (2017) *Statutory Framework for the Early Years Foundation Stage: Setting the Standards for Learning, Development and Care for Children from Birth to Five.* Available from www.gov.uk/government/publications/early-years-foundation-stage-framework-2

DfE (2019a) *Character and Resilience: A Call for Evidence.* Available from www.gov.uk/government/consultations/character-and-resilience-call-for-evidence

DfE (2019b) *Character Education Framework Guidance.* Available from www.gov.uk/government/publications/character-education-framework

DfE (2019c) *Physical Health and Mental Wellbeing.* Available from www.gov.uk/government/news/all-pupils-will-be-taught-about-mental-and-physical-wellbeing

DfE (2019d) *Relationships Education, Relationships and Sex Education (RSE) and Health Education: Statutory Guidance for Governing Bodies, Proprietors, Head Teachers, Principals, Senior Leadership Teams, Teachers.* Available from www.gov.uk/government/publications/relationships-education-relationships-and-sex-education-rse-and-health-education

DfE (2020a) *Guidance: Implementation of Relationships Education, Relationships and Sex Education and Health Education 2020–2021.* Available from www.gov.uk/government/publications/relationships-education-relationships-and-sex-education-rse-and-health-education

DfE (2020b) *Guidance: Personal, Social, Health and Economic (PSHE) Education.* Available from www.gov.uk/government/publications/personal-social-health-and-economic-education-pshe/personal-social-health-and-economic-pshe-education

DfE (2020c) *Teaching about Mental Wellbeing.* Available from www.gov.uk/guidance/teaching-about-mental-wellbeing

Her Majesty's Government (H.M. Government) (2002) *Education Act.* Available from www.legislation.gov.uk/ukpga/2002/32

House of Lords (2018) *The Ties That Bind: Citizenship and Civic Engagement in the 21st Century.* Available from https://publications.parliament.uk/pa/ld201719/ldselect/ldcitizen/118/11802.htm

Ofsted (2019) *School Inspection Handbook.* Manchester: Ofsted publications.

PSHE Association (2020) *Programme of Study for PSHE Education: Key Stages 1–5.* Available from www.pshe-association.org.uk/curriculum-and-resources/resources/programme-study-pshe-education-key-stages-1-5

Welsh Government (2020) *Curriculum for Wales.* Available from https://hwb.gov.wales/curriculum-for-wales

UNICEF (1989) *UN Convention on the Rights of the Child U.K.* Available from www.unicef.org.uk/what-we-do/un-convention-child-rights/

www.afpe.org.uk/physical-education/2014-national-curriculum/

www.gov.uk/government/news/national-citizen-service

www.gov.scot/policies/girfec/wellbeing-indicators-shanarri/

www.napce.org.uk

www.smscqualitymark.org.uk

www.wholeeducation.org

# Chapter 6

# Creating a healthy ethos and environment

The previous chapter looked at the current curriculum, which, despite the difficulties of having too much prescription and a surfeit of rigorous assessment, has taken a step forward in giving greater focus to the importance of both physical and mental health. This chapter is concerned with how to create an environment, both inside and outside an educational setting, which is conducive to supporting the wellbeing of all who learn and work there.

## Establishing the right ethos

A document referred to earlier in this book, which was commissioned by PHE and written on behalf of the Children and Young People's Mental Health Coalition (CYPMHC), sets out eight principles that can be used to promote the emotional health and wellbeing of students in schools and colleges (Public Health England, 2015).

### Eight principles for promoting emotional health and wellbeing

After recognising that the principles build on what many schools and colleges are already doing, each chapter investigates one of the eight principles and poses a key question. In essence, the key questions and chapter contents can be summarised as follows:

1    Leadership and management

How is the school or college providing visible senior leadership for emotional health and wellbeing?

Leadership and management is seen as the central tenet, around which the other principles revolve. The use of the word 'visible' is important, as it makes it clear that, while everyone must be involved in giving emotional wellbeing the prominence it deserves, it is very hard to make an impact without the support and backing of the SLT.

2    School ethos and environment

> How does the school or college's culture promote respect and value diversity?

This refers to the physical, social and emotional environment in which staff and students spend much of the week and which will affect their physical and emotional wellbeing. Critical for this are the relationships between staff, and between staff and students.

3    Curriculum, teaching and learning

> What focus is given within the curriculum to social and emotional learning and promoting personal resilience, and how is learning assessed?

Written before health education became a compulsory subject, this highlights the importance of using the PSHE curriculum and other opportunities to promote resilience and support social and emotional learning (as illustrated in previous chapters).

4    Student voice

> How does the school or college ensure all students have the opportunity to express their views and influence decisions?

Involving students in making the decisions that affect them is known to have a positive impact on their emotional health. In addition to recognising this to be the case, there need to be mechanisms in place to ensure that students' views can and do have an impact.

5    Staff development, health and wellbeing

> How are staff supported in relation to their own health and wellbeing and able to support student wellbeing?

An integral principle of a whole-school approach is that staff are supported as well as students, both through SLT making sure workloads are as manageable as possible and through staff being able to access support. In addition, they need to have opportunities to increase their understanding of young people's mental health issues through ongoing access to training.

6    Identifying need and monitoring impact

> How does the school or college assess the needs of students and the impact of interventions to improve wellbeing?

This covers assessment tools, such as the SDQ mentioned previously, as a basis for assessing mental health needs and knowing what kind of support students need. Also mentioned are: the Stirling Children's Wellbeing Scale, developed by the Stirling EPS, and the Warwick–Edinburgh Mental Wellbeing Scale (https://warwick.ac.uk/fac/sci/med/research/platform/wemwbs/).

7    Working with parents/ carers

> How does the school or college work in partnership with parents and carers to promote emotional health and wellbeing?

As the family is fundamental to a young person's wellbeing, it is suggested that, in addition to working in partnership with families in terms of involving them in their child's education and more generally in the life of the school, providing or signposting support for parenting skills and understanding emotional well-being will be beneficial to everyone.

8    Targeted support

> How does the school or college ensure timely and effective identifica-tion of students who would benefit from targeted support and ensure appropriate referral to support services?

The final principle concentrates on young learners who are more likely to need targeted support, such as those who are in care, those who are themselves young carers, and those living in households that are not conducive to their wellbeing. Early identification and getting them the support they need is seen as improving their chances of overcoming any difficulties. The AcSEED Award is mentioned as having been founded by young people who have experienced mental illness and is presented to schools which have made a significant effort to support the mental health of their students.

In summary, the eight principles might be said to be about how the right ethos and environment stems from the way the setting is led and managed. This includes:

- How the learning in the school promotes resilience and emotional learning
- How the wellbeing of staff, students and their families is addressed
- How students' needs are identified and targeted support is sought

Having had that broad focus on getting the right overall ethos and environment in which mental health and wellbeing can flourish, the next approaches look more specifically at wellbeing, beginning with the eight wellbeing factors that make up the approach to wellbeing in Scotland.

## Getting it right for every child (GIRFEC)

Since 2006, the Scottish Government has developed an approach which encourages partnership working between families and those who work with them (Scottish Government, 2006). Known as 'Getting it right for every child' (GIRFEC) the approach is based on children's rights and reflects the UNCRC, which has been mentioned elsewhere in this book. In addition, it is also concerned with the rights of parents, as stated in the European Convention on the Exercise of Children's Rights (Council of Europe, 1996).

The GIRFEC approach has been tested and developed across Scotland to be:

- Child-focused
- Based on an understanding of the wellbeing of a child in their current situation
- Based on tackling needs early
- Requiring joined-up working

Within the wellbeing theme, there are eight wellbeing factors which support children and young people so that they can grow up feeling loved, safe and respected and can realise their full potential. These eight factors are often referred to by their initial letters – SHANARRI. They can be used as wellbeing indicators, which make it easier for children, families and the people working with them to discuss how a child or young person is doing at a given point in time and to highlight if there is a need for support. It is accepted that there is no set level of wellbeing that children should achieve, as every child will be influenced by individual experiences and changing needs as they grow older. These factors are used across the services that work with children and families.

SHANARRI is illustrated by a wheel, at the centre of which is the need to give every child the 'Best start in life: Ready to succeed'. Around the edge of the wheel are the terms: confident individuals, effective contributors, responsible citizens, successful learners. The eight factors, which flow from the central tenet, are depicted as segments of the wheel. Schools in Scotland make use of the SHANARRI wellbeing indicators to assess the overall wellbeing of a child using these descriptors:

| | |
|---|---|
| *S* – **SAFE** | Protected from abuse, neglect or harm at school, at home and in the community |
| *H* – **HEALTHY** | Having the highest attainable standards in physical and mental health, as well as access to health care. This also includes support in making healthy and safe choices |
| *A* – **ACHIEVING** | Being supported and guided in their learning and in the development of their skills, confidence and self-esteem – at home, at school and in the community |
| *N* – **NURTURED** | Having a nurturing place to live, in a family setting with additional help as needed |
| *A* – **ACTIVE** | Having opportunities to take part in activities such as play, recreation and sport. This contributes to healthy growth and development at home and in the community |

*R – RESPECTED*      Having the opportunity to be heard and involved in the decisions that affect them

*R – RESPONSIBLE*    Having opportunities and encouragement to play active roles in their school and community

*I – INCLUDED*       Having opportunities to overcome social, educational, physical and economic inequalities and being accepted in the community in which they live and learn

An example of a school using SHANARRI is Baltasound Junior High School the most northerly school in the UK on the Island of Unst in the Shetland Islands. Despite its small size and its remoteness, the island is full of interest and activities for its inhabitants. Among many other features, there are two nature reserves, one of which is home to 25,000 pairs of puffins each summer; a heritage centre, prehistoric standing stones and Viking houses; a boat museum and a leisure centre with a swimming pool; and clubs for sailing, rowing, football, netball, badminton, squash and many other sports.

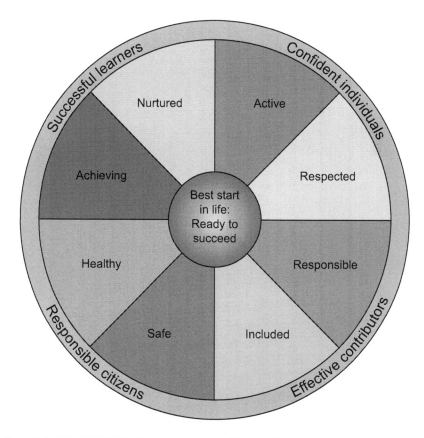

*Figure 6.1* SHANARRI Wheel (www.gov.scot/publications)

The school is as far north as southern Greenland and the nearest city is Bergen in Norway. To reach Lerwick, the main town in the Shetland Islands, entails a two-hour journey on two ferries. The head teacher of Baltasound School is Paul Thomson, who, like many others on the island, has to take on additional roles. In his case he is also a firefighter with the Scottish Fire and Rescue Service.

## Case study   Baltasound Junior High School

This school has classes for nursery children through to secondary students who can stay until they are 16. When they leave, they may move on to Anderson High School or Shetland College, or into employment. The school is very much part of the island community with students, staff and parents all working closely together. The school has both a Pupil Council and a Parent Council.

The school's core themes and values are:

- Our community and volunteering
- Outdoors and the environment
- Opportunities for everyone
- Celebrating what makes us unique

At the centre of a diagrammatic model of the school curriculum the eight factors of SHANARRI are set out in the centre, illustrating how these principles are central to all areas of the school's work.

Health and wellbeing has an important place in the curriculum. It encompasses physical, mental, emotional and social wellbeing and aims to enable students to establish a pattern of health and wellbeing that will be sustained into adult life. Each term there is a focus on an area of health and wellbeing, such as healthy eating or physical exercise (including the daily mile for primary classes), which becomes a focus throughout the school. Full use is also made of the variety of terrains, from sandy beaches to soaring cliffs.

Paul points out that the school may be small and in a far-flung corner of the UK, but that does not limit his ambition for his students. In the entrance to the school are photographs of former students and what they went on to do. Paul says:

In recent years we have had examples of professional sportspeople (representing Scotland at the Commonwealth Games), geologists, teachers, volunteers in the 3rd sector, quantity surveyors and more. This matches our school motto and the fact that we can do anything and be anyone. Being rural and remote does not hold us back, far from it – it's what makes us unique and we are proud to celebrate that.

Although on the small side for the age range it covers and being cut off from the facilities of less isolated school settings, here is an example of how a school has turned its location into an advantage and offered a curriculum that has encouraged pupils to take the direction that suits them.

### Digital 5 A Day

There have been many references throughout this book to the NHS 'Five steps/ ways to wellbeing' (NHS, 2020), which, in common with SHANARRI, goes across the services working with children and young people. More recently, the NHS has added some 'do nots' to the first three of the five steps people should take. In short, the suggestions are:

| | | |
|---|---|---|
| 1 | Connect with other people, | but do not rely on technology and social media alone to build relationships |
| 2 | Be physically active, | but do not feel you have to spend hours in the gym. |
| 3 | Learn new skills | but do not feel this means taking new qualifications or exams. |

Along similar lines, the Children's Commissioner for England, Anne Long-field, produced a digital version, which is primarily a guide for parents. Its aim is to show them how they can help their children enjoy the benefits of the online world, without, as she explains, being totally consumed by it. Longfield says:

> Taken as a whole, and supplemented with parents own ideas about what they want for their children, I hope the '5 A Day' will be at the very least a starting point for parents to tackle one of the modern parenting world's newest and biggest dilemmas and help children to lead the way as active digital citizens.
>
> (Children's Commissioner for England, 2017)

Here are her suggestions:

| | | |
|---|---|---|
| 1 | *Connect* | Use the internet to stay connected to friends and family members, and to socialise safely |
| 2 | *Be active* | Make use of online resources to get moving and boost emotional wellbeing |
| 3 | *Get creative* | Use digital tools to learn, build new skills and discover new passions |

4    *Give to others*    Stay positive and support others throughout the digital day
5    *Be mindful*       If parents are feeling worried by coronavirus, a children's
                        guide to the virus helps explain the situation

Another variation has been to look at happiness rather than wellbeing, where
ten keys, rather than five steps, have been identified.

### Ten steps towards school staff wellbeing

These come from the Anna Freud National Centre for Children and Families.
As mentioned in the previous chapter, it is no good concentrating on pupils'
wellbeing without thinking about the wellbeing of staff. The ten steps come in
the form of ten questions, which have been summarised as follows:

1   Is there a mental health lead for staff?
2   Is there a mental health policy addressing the needs of staff?
3   How does the ethos of the school promote openness about mental
    wellbeing?
4   Are there opportunities for supervision to support staff in taking decisions
    about pupils' mental health?
5   Do staff know how to access supervision outside the line management
    structure?
6   Could measures be trialled to reduce workload and does the SLT lead by
    example in, for example, limiting emails out of hours?
7   Is there a dedicated area where staff can take time out if needed?
8   Are there opportunities for staff to participate in activities with colleagues
    which are not linked to their work?
9   Is it feasible to introduce a staff wellbeing survey?
10  Is the mental wellbeing of staff an agenda item at staff and governor
    meetings?

### Ten keys to happier living

The idea of identifying '10 Keys to Happier Living' comes from 'Action for
Happiness', which is a charity that describes itself as a movement of people
committed to building a happier and more caring society, where people care
less about what they can get for themselves and more about the happiness of
others. It says it has no religious, political or commercial affiliations. It was
founded in 2010 by three people: Lord Richard Layard, Professor of Economics
at the London School of Economics and author of books on the subject; Geoff
Mulgan, who co-chairs a World Economic Forum group looking at innovation
and entrepreneurship in the fourth industrial revolution; and Sir Anthony Seldon, whose work on introducing Happiness Lessons at Wellington College was
mentioned earlier. The patron is the Dalai Lama, who describes living more

compassionately and putting the happiness of others at the centre of our lives, as 'the path to peace and happiness' (see 'Action for Happiness' (2010) website under 'Our Patron').

The first five keys are based on the Five steps to wellbeing and are said to be about how we interact with the outside world in our daily activities. Put in a different order, they spell out the word 'GREAT'.

| | |
|---|---|
| Giving | Do things for others |
| Relating | Connect with people |
| Exercising | Taking care of your body |
| Awareness | Live life mindfully |
| Trying out | Keep learning new things |

The second five keys are described as coming from inside us and depend on our attitude to life. They spell out the word '**DREAM**'.

| | |
|---|---|
| Direction | Have goals to look forward to |
| Resilience | Find ways to bounce back |
| Emotions | Look for what's good |
| Acceptance | Be comfortable with who you are |
| Meaning | Be part of something bigger |

According to 'Action for Happiness', our genes influence about 50% of the variation in our personal happiness; our circumstances, (such as income and environment) affect only about 10%. This means that as much as 40% is accounted for by our daily activities and the conscious choices we make. In other words, our actions really can make a difference. 'Action for Happiness' has associated non-profit partner organisations in Australia, Germany, Italy and Czech Republic. All these ideas about how to improve emotional wellbeing and happiness have much in common and, between them, they give some clear pointers about the ethos educational settings might provide.

## Creating the right environment

Moving on from the ethos needed to create the right environment for good mental health and emotional wellbeing, there is the question of providing the right physical environment as well. The next case study is a school in Wales which had the opportunity to create a purpose-built environment.

### Case study of Ysgol y Deri

Ysgol y Deri is part of the Penarth Learning Community in the Vale of Glamorgan, Wales. It was built as part of the twenty-first-century-schools investment programme. It brings together on one site St Cyres Comprehensive School;

Ysgol y Deri, a special school; and Ty Deri, a small respite and residential provision. Chris Britten, the head teacher, describes his pupils as being 'differently able' and the staff he employs as having a 'can do' attitude in order to meet the wide range of needs of pupils aged 3 to 19. These include pupils with profound and multiple learning difficulties (PMLD) through to those who have a diagnosis of Asperger's syndrome and are working towards GCSEs and A levels, but whose exceptionally high levels of anxiety have been a barrier to learning in their local schools.

The school uses 'positive behaviour management', which moves away from a negative, punitive approach, and 'functional behaviour analysis', which is another way of looking at the adjustments that can be made to produce a change in behaviour rather than being confrontational. In line with trauma-informed schools holding the TISUK award, the school sees positive relationships and connectedness as essential prerequisites for enabling children to learn. (TISUK's training is highlighted in the DfE (2018) advice on mental health and behaviour in schools, as supporting and promoting positive mental health.) For measuring both pupils' wellbeing and engagement during some activities, the 'Leuven 5 point scale' is used. This was developed at the Research Centre for Experimental Education at Leuven University in Belgium and is used in the UK, particularly for children at an early developmental stage.

## Case study   Ysgol y Deri

The school is underpinned by a range of interventions that ensure pupils are regulated and 'ready to learn'.

The school has a Behaviour Support Team, where the emphasis is on *support*. In addition, a number of ELSAs deliver both group and one-to-one sessions. ELSAs receive intensive training from EPs to support a whole range of emotional needs in the school, including:

- Emotional awareness
- Self-esteem
- Anger management
- Social and friendship skills
- Loss and bereavement

The school recognises that pupils learn better when they are happier and their emotional needs are being met, and ELSAs are a key part of this. Learning coaches help pupils to choose appropriate pathways and assist in transitions between Key Stages and also between school and FE.

A sensory approach to learning is fundamental for many pupils, in order to help them make sense of the world. The sensory curriculum includes activities that develop vision, hearing, touch, taste, smell and movement/balance, either in isolation or as part of a multi-sensory approach. The occupational therapists (OTs) produce 'sensory profiles' for many pupils, particularly for those who have autism.

Due to the very wide range of pupils at the school, and being very conscious of the need to foster their emotional wellbeing, the school uses a wide range of approaches and interventions.

The school's Intervention Programme runs out of the Launch Pad room and works in conjunction with the Behaviour Support Team, class teachers, occupational therapists (OTs) speech and language therapists (SaLTs), play therapists and music therapists to provide pupils with the skills needed to re-engage with their education. An Intervention Panel meets every half-term to assess progress, prioritise new referrals and to plan the interventions for each pupil. These may be for short sessions or for day-long experiences, when a range of activities is designed to build confidence and self-esteem. In addition to those listed previously, other interventions include:

| | |
|---|---|
| Aromatherapy | Massaging the hands and/ or feet using essential oils is known to have a calming effect |
| Immersive environment | This uses virtual reality, as in Star Trek's 'Holodeck' |
| Magic carpet | This device from Poland is an interactive projection tool which can be used on the floor or table |
| Rebound therapy | Internationally recognised, it was founded in the 1970s as a specific model of trampoline therapy, as opposed to using the trampoline for physical sequences of increasing complexity. It combines therapeutic exercise with enjoyment and is taught by those who have been trained by accredited providers |
| Touch Therapy | The school is known as a Centre of Excellence in Touch Therapy and many of the staff have been trained to deliver sessions in the school's Touch Therapy room, which has an integrated sound and light system. This pioneering therapy gives pupils opportunities for relaxation, positive communication, empathy and wellbeing and uses all the senses to establish a sense of worth and enjoyment |
| Yoga | Regular yoga practice gently rests the nervous system, creating a feeling of calm and an ability to cope better with others and the environment around the young learner, whether feeling stressed, having too much or too little energy, or being in a disorganised state. |

Although few schools and settings may be in a position to have the facilities to offer the range of approaches and therapies that Ysgol y Deri provides, the case study confirms the different types of support young people may need and highlights the importance of focusing on emotional wellbeing whether a child has complex cognitive difficulties or has considerable academic potential.

### Free schools

As the pupil population has grown, free schools have been one way of meeting demand. Many are in deprived areas and are seen by the government as giving disadvantaged pupils access to greater choices. Free schools can be set up by charities, groups of teachers, existing schools or parents. They can be primary, secondary, all-through or 16 to 19. They can also be specifically for pupils who need a different environment, such as free special schools for pupils with different types of SEND, or AP academies for pupils who need alternative provision because they have medical needs, or have been, or are likely to be, excluded.

The next case study features another school designed from scratch for a specific population and one where both the indoor and outdoor environment had to be developed.

### Case study of Church Lawton school

Church Lawton school is a free special school for autistic pupils. The National Autistic Society (NAS) has been providing autism-specific education since the 1960s. When free schools became an option, with the charity acting as sponsor, the NAS Academies Trust was established to own and manage its free schools. In 2015, Church Lawton School was the second free school it opened. Not many may have the opportunity to design their provision from scratch, but that was what happened in the case of Church Lawton, which was designed to meet the needs of autistic pupils. After designing the building and being satisfied that it provided an effective working atmosphere for pupils and staff, everyone's attention was turned to improving the outdoor area where, although they were fortunate to have plenty of ground, staff and pupils needed to plan how to maximise its use.

## Case study    Church Lawton School, Stoke-on-Trent

Church Lawton is a special free school for 64 pupils aged 4 to 19 who have a diagnosis of autism, an EHCP and live in the area of East Cheshire, Staffordshire, Stoke or neighbouring authorities.

The school was purpose-built. The rooms have a lot of natural light along with LED dimmable lighting, noise absorption panels were built into ceilings and walls throughout, and there are spacious low-arousal corridors. There are individual learning areas in every classroom and each opens onto an outside area. There is a learning centre for children with more complex needs and a nurture class where lessons are kept to 20 minutes. Children with a particular gift for a subject can study it at an appropriate level, including taking GCSE exams early.

After much fundraising, the Sport and Sensory Field was opened recently. In addition to an all-weather surface for badminton, basketball, hockey, football, cricket or tennis, features include:

- For touch: plants, different gravel surfaces and barefoot walks
- For movement: scooters, tricycles, bikes for towing and go-karts (all of which require communication) and a cycle path
- A wooden viewing gallery overlooking the sports pitch kitted out with picnic-style tables, so it can be used for outdoor lessons and breaktime chats
- A life skills hut where students can practise making beds, setting a table and preparing tea and toast.

The school is a proponent of outdoor Adventure Education. Activities offered include: climbing, skiing, bush craft, horseback riding, orienteering, camping, sailing and canoeing.

The principal, Paul Scales, says:

> Autistic students can experience sensory overload. As well as creating a comfortable, quiet and spacious place to learn inside the school, Adventure Education involves collaborative learning experiences with a high level of physical (and often emotional) challenge. Practical problem-solving, explicit reflection and discussion of thinking and emotion may also be involved.

The emotional wellbeing of everyone at the school is an integral part of what the school does and contributes significantly to a calm and considerate ethos. There is a very active Wellbeing Team and staff can identify wellbeing concerns of students through referral sheets kept in the staff room. Every child has a learning mentor who supports them, helps them to carry out their programme, and keeps in touch with families.

The school was recently successful with an Erasmus + (EU) application for KS4 and Post-16 students under a programme called 'Getting ready for adult life'. The project involves Church Lawton teachers and pupils linking with pupils who have Asperger's syndrome or high-performing autism – the terms used by the Erasmus + programme, rather than the school or charity – and attend Rodengymnasiet in Norrtälje, Sweden. To travel, spend time away from home and meet new people are opportunities to practise the skills of self-management and social interaction. The objective is to raise self-confidence through real-life challenges which are outside students' comfort zones and are supported by both sets of staff.

### International links

In common with Church Lawton, the next case study school has both strong international links and an emphasis on pupils helping to create a better environment indoors and outside for their school community.

### Case study of Waunarlwydd Primary School

Waunarlwydd is a primary school in Swansea and is part of the North Gower Partnership, which is a long-standing collaboration between the feeder schools to Gowerton Comprehensive School. The school has been one of the pioneer schools, helping to develop a new curriculum that starts in 2022 (Welsh Government, 2020). This will include a focus on the physical, psychological, emotional and social aspects of life. One of the six areas of learning and experience is 'health and wellbeing'. Ruth Davies, the head teacher, says:

> We are a community which believes strongly in the value of building positive relationships. The safety and well-being of our children are some of our priority aims. Our team works collaboratively to provide an environment which allows pupils to feel safe and well-cared for, as it is our belief that this remains a pre-requisite for progress and achievement.

### Case study   Waunarwlydd Primary School

The school takes pupils from the age of 3, but toddlers from Plant Bach Pre-school are invited to join the Nursery class for an hour each week, to help them prepare for school.

To help children develop leadership and management skills, every child in KS2 applies to be part of one of ten Senedd groups. (In Wales, there is no separate KS1 as the foundation stage is extended until KS2.)

The school has ten Senedd groups, which grew out of the school's work as a Rights Respecting School. These groups meet regularly to discuss ideas for improving their chosen area of the school. Each Senedd group elects a Chair, who meets with the head or deputy head, every half-term, to update them on their action plans. These ten chairpersons form the school council.

At the first meeting of the *Eco Senedd*, the children developed their mission statement:

We will make our school clean and green, Together we are the eco team.

Since then, they have worked with the rest of the school community to sow seeds and to plant trees and shrubs, as well as conducting environmental surveys. Under the slogan: Reduce, Reuse, Recycle, an assortment of articles, such as batteries, toothpaste tubes and brushes, writing equipment and crisp packets have all been collected and recycled.

The Healthy Schools Senedd designed a healthy lunchbox leaflet for parents and has created zones in the playground to promote a healthy body and mind.

The school has a number of links with schools across the UK and internationally. One of these is through 'Comenius' (https://uk.april-international.com/en/exchange-programmes/comenius-programme) which is a project funded by the British Council. It enables schools to work collaboratively on a sustainable development project and to find out about approaches to sustainable development in other countries. A by-product of this partnership is the opportunity to learn about different cultures and traditions through email and 'snail mail' exchanges between pupils. Another British Council funded project, 'Connecting Classrooms' linked Waunarlwydd with schools in Trinidad and Tobago. Pupils shared projects and explained their country's history, cultures and traditions. Through the Welsh Assembly, the Chongqing-Wales Partnership has enabled many schools in Swansea to have a direct link with this south-west area of China.

The school has gained the International School Award, partly as a result of its work as a 'Rights Respecting School'. At Waunarlwydd, there are eight core rights which are at the heart of the school's ethos:

1    The right to know our rights
2    The right to learn
3    The right to play
4    The right to be safe
5    The right to be heard
6    The right to be healthy
7    The right to our own beliefs
8    The right to a name

The school ambassadors' scheme is run in primary schools across Wales. Two children are elected by the other pupils in each school to be ambassadors. The ambassador's role is to:

•    Inform children in their school about the Children's Commissioner for Wales
•    Inform children in their school all about children's rights and the United Nations Convention on the Rights of the Child (UNICEF, 1989)
•    Work alongside the school council to find out what children in the school think could be improved and then work with other people in the school to change things

In addition to other developments already mentioned, the school has a woodland walk, which provides all classes with first-hand experiences and opportunities to problem-solve as part of outdoor education.

## Outdoor learning

It was Confucius (551–479 bc) who is reported to have said:

> I hear and I forget
> I see and I remember
> I do and I understand

Although plenty of practical learning can, and does, go in in classrooms, the outdoor environment lends itself to hands-on experiences and the development of physical skills. Outdoor learning is about more than taking outside what could happen indoors.

### Learning Outside the Classroom (LOtC)

The organisation, LOtC, defines outdoor learning as using places other than the classroom for teaching and learning. As well as school grounds, it suggests that this can include:

- Local woods, parks or nature reserves
- Museums, theatres, galleries, libraries and archives
- City farms, farms, the countryside and community gardens
- Zoos and botanical gardens
- Heritage and cultural sites
- Language and fieldwork visits
- Field study and environmental centres
- Remote wild and adventurous places
- Expeditions abroad

People who are champions of LoTC include the Duke of Edinburgh; Richard Branson; and the presenter, explorer and naturalist, Paul Rose, who writes on the organisation's website:

> I shone at three things in school – trips away from school, sports and metalwork. Those classrooms were not for me: overheated, incomprehensible and dull lessons. I was so bored. Then, when I was fourteen, my geography teacher took us outside of the classroom and all the horrors that it held for me. I shall never forget how alive and in tune with nature I felt.

### Learning Through Landscapes

In common with LOtC a UK charity, 'Learning Through Landscapes', which specialises in outdoor learning and play in educational settings, is also well supported. Its patrons include David Attenborough and Jonathan Porritt, the sustainability campaigner, writer and advocate of the Green Party. On its website is 'The Good School Playground Guide', with a foreword by the Chief Medical Officer for Scotland and illustrations of playgrounds throughout the UK and further afield. 'Learning Through Landscapes' is a founder member of the International School Grounds Alliance (ISGA), which works across Europe, North America, Africa and Australasia.

### Forest School

One branch of outdoor education is Forest School, a movement that is now popular across much of the UK, Germany and Scandinavia.

---

## Information point   History of Forest School

| | |
|---|---|
| 1970s/80s | Building on a long history of outdoor education, the Forest School movement emerged |
| 1990s | After a visit to Denmark and its preschool system's open-air culture, a group of nursery nurses from the UK started a Forest School for preschool children. Soon Forest School was being offered across the UK. |
| 2000s | Shortly after the turn of the century, a national conference led to a UK definition, saying that it helped to: 'develop confidence and self-esteem, through hands-on learning experiences in a local woodland environment'. |
| 2010s | Six guiding principle were agreed upon, which included the need for frequent and regular sessions in a wooded environment where children could make choices and be supported to take risks, with qualified practitioners being in charge (www.forestschoolassociation.org) |

---

### Case study of Belmont School

The following case study is of Belmont School in Harrow, London, which is an accredited Forest School. For many pupils and families, their homes and community do not have the space or opportunity to explore an outside world of woodland or natural environment. This has been a significant reason why Belmont has developed as a Forest School, accredited by the National Forest School Association.

This move was identified as an important and integral part of the school's development and was enabled by the appointment, in 2016, of an assistant head who now has two days a week leadership time, including that for Forest School. This decision and appointment of a fully accredited Forest School trainer has been so successful that the school is now a much sought after provider of formal and informal support and training to develop Forest Schools nationally, and internationally. Teachers have visited Belmont from countries as far away as China, South Korea and Australia. This has led to two additional members of staff being trained as Forest School teachers.

## Case study    Belmont School

Belmont is a multi-cultural primary school in Harrow. It is part of a diverse community and celebrates the achievements of all learners, focusing not just on academic success but also sporting and creative achievements.

The aim of Forest School at Belmont is for pupils to enjoy and respect the outside world, with Forest School activities being seen as 'transformational'. The younger pupils have a weekly opportunity for Forest School activities, at school or nearby, while older pupils have regular visits and school journeys, too.

The activities encourage independence in all areas of life, as it is important that there are opportunities for children to learn to manage their own risks. This is achieved, for example, by allowing children of all ages to use tools, light fires, build dens and climb trees. These activities develop the ability to solve real-world issues, build self-belief and prepare young learners to take supported risks. In this way, Forest School helps participants to become, healthy, resilient, creative and independent learners.

The school also actively encourages families to engage wherever possible in Forest School activities, so they too can experience what Forest School offers.

In the school's vision it states that:

> Our curriculum is enhanced to ensure that children's learning is relevant, builds on their experiences and provides them with the skills they need to support them in later life.

The school believes Forest School helps create such opportunities.

Belmont has an interesting document on its website called 'Mental health promotion at Belmont School', which shows how other policies, including: Anti-bullying; Learning policy; Supporting pupils with medical needs; E-safety and acceptable user policy; Suicide and self-harm; and PSHE, combine to form part of promoting mental health across the school. The use of the SDQ, Revised Children's Anxiety and Depression Scale (RCADS) and Conners Scale, means that, together with other relevant information everything can be recorded in one place, ('CPOMS'- a Safeguarding Software for Schools). This, in turn, enables the school to target early intervention strategies and support, as well as aiming to prevent emotional and behaviour problems, both in school and in the home, through:

1   Staff trained in identifying changes in behaviour that indicate emotional distress
2   Good home/school links to ensure any family changes are communicated
3   Strategies to support children when emotionally distressed

In common with other schools already mentioned, the school is recognised as a 'Rights Respecting School'.

### An outdoor curriculum

The final case study is about a school which is not a Forest School, but has developed its grounds with the pupils in order to increase its curriculum offer.

### Case study of Oak Grove College

Oak Grove College is in Worthing, West Sussex. It is part of a federation with three other schools: Cornfield, Herons Dale and Palatine. The school has made the most of its grounds to offer a wide range of learning opportunities to its pupils. The head teacher, Phillip Potter, says:

> The college's creative approaches to learning mean that many off-site visits are undertaken, the grounds are used extensively, and there is a practical approach to the curriculum, including our commitment and dedication to The Arts as a vehicle for the development of self-esteem.

## Case study    Oak Grove College, West Sussex

Oak Grove is a special school for around 260 pupils. It is a secondary day school with Post-16 provision. A wide range of pupils includes those who have moderate learning difficulties (MLD), severe learning difficulties (SLD) and profound and multiple learning difficulties (PMLD).

Learning through making is a fully integrated part of the students' educational experience, including practical activities on the school grounds. Working alongside staff and volunteers, students have developed, landscaped and planted the grounds themselves. By using the outdoors as a resource for all subjects, be it literacy and numeracy, science or art, students are able to work with nature, understand the different seasons and what it means to design and alter, and care for and respect, their own environment.

Groups from other schools and local businesses, young adult mentors, parents and carers, all come to work at the school, making outdoor learning a real community project. The school has hosted Concordia, an international charity based in Brighton, which, since the 1940s, has linked volunteers to short-term projects in different countries. (Concordia is also a Delivery Partner for the NCS, which is described more fully in Chapter 5 of this book.) The grounds have been opened as part of the National Garden Scheme and the school has participated in Worthing Allotment Society's Annual Show.

The school believes that integration into the wider community and working alongside others, is a vital aspect of preparing for adult life. Year 10 and 11 students spend a day a week at three placements during the year – Northbrook College, Brinsbury College and the SAND Project, where a number of options is open to them, including travel training, catering and PE.

In addition to outdoor learning, Oak Grove, together with Herons Dale and Palatine schools, were part of a pilot for the Therapies in Schools service (www.outdoor-learning.org/). This has been funded by West Sussex County Council and delivered by Sussex Community NHS Trust. The TIS service works collaboratively with the existing therapy provision in the school to provide a 'one team therapy approach'. This has enabled schools, families and therapists to work in partnership so that pupils' educational and therapeutic needs are blended. The TIS service is now available to special schools across West Sussex. Additional therapists have been employed, who work alongside education staff so that they can provide personalised therapeutic input for their pupils. TIS delivers an accredited, modular training programme in three streams:

- Sensory processing
- Life skills
- Physical development

Each stream has three levels. TIS Level 1 training has been delivered to all the school staff involved and Level 2 is available for those who show interest in learning more advanced skills, while Level 3 creates 'Champions', who can be approached for support and advice. Parents, families and carers have also been offered Level 1 training.

Oak Grove College has two Wellbeing and Behaviour senior teachers, one for KS3 and one for KS4. In the conversation that follows, Sarah Ellis, who carries out the KS3 role, explains more about the TIS Project and how the school's outdoor learning is a central part of the school's curriculum.

*In conversation with Sarah Ellis, Wellbeing and Behaviour,*
*senior teacher for KS3*

Q. **Could you tell us about the school's involvement with the Therapy**
   **in Schools Project, funded by West Sussex CC and delivered by**
   **Sussex Community NHS Trust?**

The Therapy in Schools pilot project first emerged as a joint initiative idea
following the need to build a model of educational provision and support
in West Sussex, enabling children and young people, wherever possible, to
live and go to their local early years setting, school or college. Our special
schools needed to be able to compete with independent schools outside
the area that parents saw as providing better therapeutic support. In addition, schools reported that their staff lacked confidence in delivering phys-
iotherapy and occupational therapy programmes to children with more
complex needs and there was no training available

An important element of TIS is that they also work directly with the
whole family as well as with the young person. This means that families
feel more confident that their child's needs can be met locally and school
staff feel more confident that their training has enabled them to support
young people more effectively. The therapists offer surgeries to schools and
their staff so that they can come and talk about students and get support
and ideas for strategies. TIS is now in every special school in West Sussex
and is fully staffed.

2. **Could you say something about your school's outdoor and practi-**
   **cal learning strand?**

Our outdoor and practical learning strand is now known as Vocational
Learning and involves a unit on enterprise. It includes Design Technology,
Food Technology, Gardening and Enterprise.

These practical subjects are amongst the most popular with our MLD
students and our aim is to build the confidence in students to leave us and
go on to FE college to study these subjects. All subject-specific learners
in KS3 have these lessons on a rotational basis throughout the year, and
they are offered as options for KS4 learners. In KS4 different accredita-
tions are followed in order to give the students access to FE and to mark
their achievements. These include the Jamie Oliver Home Cooking Skills
BTEC and The Prince's Trust qualifications. The percentage of young
people with SEND in West Sussex who find employment after finishing
education is very low. We are committed to encouraging our learners to
look to the future and aim for employment. This is becoming increasingly
successful.

The whole school uses the garden. We have a sensory area which our
subject-specific learners have created for our PMLD learners and the pathways have been completed with the students to allow access for all. Our
SLD learners also have gardening lessons with our specialist teachers and

use the garden for social communication, working together to grow, harvest and cook vegetables as well as a few sausages on the bonfire. Produce from the garden is used within the catering lessons and any excess is sold to staff to raise money for small projects within the garden.

We have constructed an outdoor cooking area, which as well as giving additional cooking space, means in the summer we can run an outside café during the annual Sixth Form Plant Sale. This is a large work-related learning project undertaken by our sixth-form students, to grow all sorts of flora in our polytunnels and these are then sold to the public across two weeks. The money raised has gone on many different things across the years, including the outdoor gym equipment.

More recently, the garden has become a place of solace for some of our SEMH learners. Heavy work such as digging and cutting has enabled students to work through their anger enough to be able to then talk about what is going on for them. Through this, we now have a fire pit and several tree stumps have been broken down and the ground made smooth. Students have been able to see that through harnessing their emotions, positive outcomes are possible. The grounds are also used to give students space to calm down. Our pastoral officers and teachers on pastoral duty will often walk with students if they are unable to focus in a lesson. The environment offers a grounding experience as well as quiet time to reflect on choices.

3. **How does your role of Wellbeing and Behaviour senior teacher KS3 link with the Pastoral Support Team?**

A year into this new role, combined with having been the strangest year ever, it is really interesting to see the dynamics slowly changing within the college. The roles came about from our deputy head retiring and the assistant head being promoted. The restructure has saved school a considerable amount of money which is something we have to do given our deficit budget. There is a senior teacher for KS4 and together we have line-managed the Pastoral Support Team. Meeting with them on a weekly basis has meant that we have been able to identify students who are displaying worrying behaviour very quickly. As a college we use CPOMS as a behaviour recording database as well as all our contacts with home and external agencies.

With the face-to-face knowledge and data from CPOMS we have been able to instigate several interventions run by the pastoral team to target students who were in danger of exclusion. This included a breakfast club and having lunchtimes together. We wanted to make sure that the pastoral team were not always dealing with negative behaviours and that the students and staff saw them as a positive support both within lessons and during breaktimes. For example, a student was having a particularly challenging time in maths. A programme was put in place where the student started off doing one-to-one maths out of the classroom, then they were joined by a couple of other students from the class to do small group work. They then went back into class with the pastoral officer and gradually this support was reduced as they settled back in. Unfortunately, COVID happened so we didn't get to see the outcome of this.

Due to the changing needs of our MLD students, specific teaching staff have been given time each week to do one-to-one work with students. This could be if there has been an increase in negative behaviours, a change in home circumstances, friendship issues, early signs of poor mental health, or students becoming increasingly withdrawn. The decision as to who gets these places is discussed in the Pastoral Support Team meetings. We have also encouraged the team to be part of our behaviour panel meetings where we discuss students in need. Their insight and perspective are so valuable as they are able to work differently with students. Not having the title of 'teacher' can make a big difference. Listening to, acting upon and sharing information and ideas with the pastoral team has meant that their confidence has grown and they are becoming more proactive. Working on low-level disruptive behaviours has meant there has been a decrease in challenging situations.

4. **What do you think has made the most difference to the emotional wellbeing of staff or pupils?**
I think the biggest difference is in the degree of overall connectedness and a better overview of all that is going on. Staff are more willing to share their concerns, which means we can then act upon these swiftly. There is a consistency of approach and open dialogue. Both KS3 and KS4 senior teachers work closely with the safeguarding officer which means we are all aware of issues both in and out of school.

The TIS Project has had a significant effect on staff and students with the most complex needs. All staff in school have had at least Level 1 training in each of the strands and those who have wanted to, have been able to become TIS Champions in one of the three areas. This has caused a greater level of confidence across the whole staff as well as having positive outcomes for students. Where we once would have had to refer a student to an external agency to be assessed, we are now able to do this in-house. For example, we had a student arrive with us displaying challenging behaviour that disrupted learning for many. We put in several referrals to outside agencies which were all refused. However, we also used our Sensory Integration Champion and our Occupational Therapy Champion to observe the classroom behaviour and with this were able to produce a sensory diet and tailored timetable so the student could settle. The student now has one-to-one support at all times, but we are hoping that with the continued input from the Champions this may be reduced as they move up through school.

5. **Is there anything else you do which stands out in some way and others might learn from?**
Alongside the TIS Project we have also worked hard to build up good relations with other external agencies. All students with PMLD are discussed

at an annual meeting at the school, where all services come together to discuss the next steps for the young person. This has been invaluable, particularly for those students moving on from us to continuing health care.

We also now have a link with CAMHS who come to us once every half-term. The Mental Health Liaison Nurse offers slots for staff to take a young person and discuss their presentation. This Tier 2 intervention acts almost like a triage for CAMHS as we are able to discuss the likelihood of the young person needing to be seen at Tier 3. They also offer advice and signpost resources that we may have not been aware of. This has been particularly successful where students have presented with some worrying behaviours which could have been the result of adverse childhood experiences (ACE). We are also able to email or call the nurse if we need some advice or information. We require parental consent for these discussions, but it is a professionals meeting. The nurse is able to discuss what she knows with the Tier 3 team, which can speed up the referral process where needed.

Staff CPD is really important to us and all new members of staff undertake an induction programme. This includes a behaviour and wellbeing session, where the senior teachers go through the expectations of all members of the community, but also some of the many reasons a behaviour may be shown. This has had positive feedback and CPD sessions have been held to discuss ACEs, therapeutic language, brain development and trauma. This has led to staff wanting to talk about their own experiences with senior leaders, but also a greater understanding of what is going on for individuals.

This year we began the process of achieving the School Mental Health Award from the Carnegie School at Leeds Beckett University. We wanted something that could give a structure to what we already did, but also guide us to be even better. Our initial assessment of this was just before lockdown and we achieved 'embracing' status. We are looking to be 'excelling' and, through the work that is being done with our students with PMLD on their mental health, we hope to gain this next year.

We also have a wellbeing steering group made up of staff from the different areas of school. It is open to anyone and is a place where issues can be raised, discussed and then hopefully a solution found to help support staff. One of our Management Committee members also attends in case there is anything at governor level that can be done. Governors are visible at school and very approachable. This gives staff the confidence to know that the school is being led by those who understand its complexities and difficulties as well as being able to celebrate our achievements.

## Conclusions

This chapter has been about the need to create the right ethos and environment, which will help to provide a welcoming place in which students and staff alike are happy to learn and work. This can prevent mental health issues developing in the first place, while recognising that, for some, other adaptations, approaches and interventions will be needed. To achieve this, the impetus needs to come from the top and permeate downwards. It is by working together that schools or colleges can achieve the right ethos, where there are no cliques or feelings of 'them and us', but everyone is on the same side and working as a team to create a place where the wellbeing of all has a chance to flourish.

The final chapter draws together the themes that have emerged throughout the book. This is followed by a section that lists all the resources that have been mentioned and where more information about them can be found.

## References

Action for Happiness (2010) *10 Keys to Happier Living*. Available from www.actionforhappiness.org/10-keys-to-happier-living

Children's Commissioner for England (2017) *Digital 5 a Day*. Available from www.childrenscommissioner.gov.uk/digital/5-a-day/

Council of Europe (1996) *European Convention on the Exercise of Children's Rights*. Available from www.coe.int/en/web/conventions/full-list/-/conventions/treaty/160

DfE (2018) *Mental Health and Behaviour in Schools: Departmental Advice for School Staff*. Available from www.gov.uk/government/publications/mental-health-and-behaviour-in-schools-2

https://uk.april-international.com/en/exchange-programmes/comenius-programme

https://warwick.ac.uk/fac/sci/med/research/platform/wemwbs/

NHS (2020) *5 Steps to Mental Well Being*. Available from www.nhs.uk/conditions/stress-anxiety-depression/improve-mental-wellbeing/

Public Health England (2015) *Promoting Children and Young People's Health and Well Being: A Whole School and College Approach*. Available from www.gov.uk/government/publications/promoting-children-and-young-peoples-emotional-health-and-wellbeing

Scottish Government (2006) *Getting It Right for Every Child*. Available from www.gov.scot/policies/girfec/

UNICEF (1989) *Rights of the Child*. UK. Available from www.unicef.org.uk/legal/cookies-and-privacy-policy/

Welsh Government (2020) *Curriculum for Wales*. Available from https://hwb.gov.wales/curriculum-for-wales

www.actionforhappiness.org

www.forestschoolassociation.org

www.outdoor-learning.org/

# Chapter 7

# A whole-school ethos
# and a range of resources

It has been fascinating to trace the steps that have led to a point where the importance of children and young people's mental health and emotional wellbeing is recognised. It has been inspiring to discover, through case studies and conversations, how much educational establishments are contributing to creating the right ethos and environment in which young learners have a chance to flourish. And it has been impressive to realise the wealth of approaches, ideas and interventions being used to provide individual support when and where it is needed. The march of progress may be slow, but there is a clear route ahead and we have to hope that all that has been promised will come to fruition, even if it takes even longer than first suggested.

This final chapter looks first at some of the themes that have emerged during the course of writing this book. Next, there is a mention of the impact of COVID-19 which happened while the book was being written. This is followed by a list of all the resources that have been mentioned and links to where they can be found. The final world goes to a student whose insight into how his life has been turned round is in the form of a poem.

## Themes that have emerged

1    Emotional wellbeing is fundamental to young learners' development and educational achievement

The first of these themes is a recognition that there is no need for a battle between academic learning and wellbeing, but an agreement that children and young people need to be in a fit state to learn before they are able to do so. In the same way that none of us is able to properly process information when in a state of heightened anxiety, young learners need to be able to concentrate on learning without being distracted or overwhelmed by other issues occurring in their lives. Having resilience as part of the curriculum will help to prevent mental health problems from developing in some pupils, while for others it will need to be supplemented by support from staff who understand their needs.

2   Behaviour should be seen primarily as a form of communication

For too long there has been an argument about the need to focus on discipline as opposed to trying to understand *why* a young person behaves in a way that is considered unacceptable. This is not to say that sanctions do not have their place, but there is a marked difference between pupils who are quite capable of following school rules but choose not to do so, and those whose behaviour should be a sign that we need to look behind, beneath and beyond the behaviour to establish its cause.

3   The voice of the child must be heard, so they are able to express their feelings and have a sense of belonging

Educational settings and other services have come a long way in making sure young people's views are listened to and influence what happens to them. In terms of emotional wellbeing, it is particularly important that they have the words and understanding to express how they feel. In addition, every young person needs to know that they are valued for who they are so they feel that vital sense of being included, of belonging to the community of which they are a part.

4   Parents and carers should be seen as co-workers in addressing mental health issues

In the same way that engaging with the views of students is known to be important, involving parents and carers as co-workers gives out the message that school and home are working together and the child knows that everyone is on the same side. Of course, there are 'hard to reach' parents, who may have their own problems, unhappy memories of school or are afraid they will be judged as being bad parents because their child is a 'problem'. They need to be reassured that the problem does not lie with their parenting skills, or in their child, but in a system that makes it hard for educational establishments to meet every young person's needs. Putting on training for parents or helping them to access it elsewhere so that they have a better understanding of their child, may make a real difference.

5   Every young people is unique and should not be expected to follow the same path, or to reach the same academic standards as others of the same age

We have an education system that tries to fit young learners into a mould, rather than allowing for different interests, aptitudes and abilities. The lack of recognition in this country for those who are good with their hands has downgraded the value of practical, hands-on learning. Yet, learning by doing is as important as learning by listening. An overemphasis on formal education before children are ready, excessive testing with the inherent danger of teaching to the test, and of overaccountability, is detrimental to the wellbeing of staff and students alike. Schools do their best to treat pupils as individuals, but the system needs to change.

6   A solution will not be reached until everyone works together across national and local government departments, across services, and across communities and charities

Throughout this book, there are many examples of what has been achieved because people came out of their silos and started working together. It is very clear how much more can be accomplished by drawing on the experience and expertise that is available in the local community, in the area, and online. On a wider scale, the more links there are across national and local government, the more joint training there is for professionals from different fields, and the more that charities form links with each other and with education, health and social care, the more that can be achieved.

The Royal Society for the Encouragement of Arts, Manufactures and Commerce, which describes itself as a global network of proactive problem solvers, said in their 'Education for the 21st Century Charter':

Education should help young people to understand how to be happy and to develop and maintain their own emotional, physical and mental well-being.

This was written before Future in Mind, before the Green Paper on Mental Health, and well before the 2020 pandemic. If it were needed then, it is even more necessary now.

## The ravages of COVID-19

It was mentioned at the start of this book that, while it was being written, COVID-19 struck. Although mental health and wellbeing issues existed long before the pandemic, they have been exacerbated by the disappearance of a way of life people were used to and the disruption this caused to young learners' education. Schools and colleges were closed or only open for some students for weeks on end. When they were opened officially, fluctuating numbers of students and staff turned up each day, depending on who was ill or having to self-isolate. When children did return to school, they faced a very different environment from the one they were used to. In addition, many experienced:

- Loss of normality and a way of life
- Bereavement and illness
- Anxiety about change and the future
- Missing time at school and with friends
- A range of family issues and concerns

When schools manage to stay open, pupils and their families may have a real concern of what the future holds and a fear of catching the virus themselves or passing it on to others. Having had to become used to periods of staying at home, some are reluctant to leave the house even when it is safe for them to do so. Pupils may worry about catching up on work they have missed and how that might affect future prospects.

Away from school, many children also worry about not knowing if there will be a job tomorrow for their parents. Not being able to meet with other family members or friends, often the source of security and comfort, has caused additional stress.

Currently, there are different rules depending on the prevalence of coronavirus in each area and country of the UK. Staff in schools and colleges have had to manage how they feel, ensure all are safe and try to support colleagues who also feel uncomfortable or worried. But, above all, they have had to reassure pupils and their families that all that can be done is being done.

Mental health and wellbeing issues may not have changed, but they have been exacerbated by a situation to which, at the time of writing, there is no end in sight.

Despite the pandemic having disastrous consequences, however, it may have provided an opportunity to rethink the testing and examination system, to consider if Ofsted in its present form is the best way of improving schools, and to look at how the bureaucracy and red tape that schools and other services are tied up in, could be substantially reduced. Then teachers would have more time to teach, students would be taught by staff who had a greater sense of wellbeing, and the ethos and environment of schools and colleges would see an improvement in the mental health and emotional wellbeing of all who work and study there.

## Finding resources

The following is a summary of the resources that have been mentioned in the book. These include approaches, interventions, materials and organisations and where they may be found. Where they include information and advice about COVID-19, this is mentioned as well.

### *Resources in alphabetical order*

*ACE* (Association for Character Education)

> The organisation supports schools, teachers and other educationalists to develop and promote character education responses that enable young people and societies to flourish.
> http://character-education.org.uk/

*Action for Happiness*

> This is a movement of people committed to building a happier and more caring society.
> www.actionforhappiness.org

*Anna Freud National Centre for Children and Families*

The centre is a child mental health research, training and treatment centre located in London, United Kingdom.
*Training and resources and COVID-19 support.*
www.annafreud.org

*Anti-Bullying Alliance*

A coalition of organisations and individuals, working together to achieve their vision to: stop bullying and create safer environments in which children and young people can live, grow, play and learn.
https://anti-bullyingalliance.org.uk/
www.nationalbullyinghelpline.co.uk/

*Anxiety UK*

UK national registered charity formed in 1970 for those affected by anxiety disorders.
www.anxietyuk.org.uk

*Books Beyond Words*

This provides books and training to people who find pictures easier to understand than words.
*COVID-19 support.*
https://booksbeyondwords.co.uk/

*Boxall Profile and online version*

This is a resource for the assessment of children and young people's social, emotional and behavioural development.
https://new.boxallprofile.org

*Butterfly Print*

Butterfly Print are specialists in design. Among other resources are some to support the SMILE wellbeing approach to the '5 ways of wellbeing'.
*COVID-19 resources.*
www.butterflyprint.co.uk/

*Centre for Mental Health*

This is a charity with over 30 years' experience in providing life-changing research, economic analysis and policy influence in mental health.
*Support for COVID-19.*
https://centreformentalhealth.org.uk

*Childline*

Online counselling service first developed by Esther Rantzen in 1986
www.childline.org.uk

*Children and Young People's Mental Health Coalition*

This is a group of charities that jointly campaign on mental health and
wellbeing issues for children and young people.
*COVID-19 support.*
www.cypmhc.org.uk

*Cognitive behaviour therapy (CBT)*

CBT is a talking therapy that can help manage problems by changing the way people think and behave. It looks for practical ways to
improve a person's state of mind on a daily basis.

*Conditional Positive Regard (CPR)*

This is providing warmth, affection, and acceptance, provided that
certain conditions, standards and/or expectations are met.

*Every Mind Matters*

This is an NHS website giving practical advice on learning more about
your own mental health, as well as how to help others.
*COVID-19 support.*
www.nhs.uk/oneyou

*Forest Schools*

Forest Schools are nature-based communities where trained practitioners nurture learner-led exploration and discovery, enabling mean-
ingful experiences for positive lifelong impacts.
www.forestschools.com

*Good Childhood Index*

The Children's Society created the Index and it measures how children in the UK feel about their lives. Their annual report examines
the latest trends in wellbeing.
www.childrenssociety.org.uk

*Heads Together*

Heads Together is a mental health initiative spearheaded by The
Royal Foundation of The Duke and Duchess of Cambridge, to
tackle stigma and change the conversation on mental health.
www.headstogether.org.uk

*Health and Wellbeing Boards*

The Boards are central to the government's vision of a more integrated approach to health and social care.
www.localgov.uk

*Healthwatch*

There is a local Healthwatch in every area of England. They try to find out what people like about services, and what could be improved, and then share these views with those with the power to make change happen.
www.healthwatch.co.uk

*Healthy London Partnership*

A very large website with many links for advice and resources.
*Advice for COVID-19.*
www.healthylondon.org/

*Kooth*

Provides a digital mental health support service that gives children and young people online access to experienced counsellors.
www.kooth.com

*Mental Health First Aid Training (MHFA)*

Details of MHFA training and Youth Mental Health First Aid (YMHFA) courses are both available on the same website.
https://mhfaengland.org/

*Mental Health Foundation*

Mental Health Foundation is an all-age charity with a major focus on prevention.
*COVID-19 resources.*
www.mentalhealth.org.uk

*Mentally Healthy Schools*

Launched as a legacy of the Heads Together campaign, the website is a collaboration between three leading child mental health and education charities. It provides free information and practical resources for UK schools and FE settings.
*COVID-19 resources.*
www.mentallyhealthyschools.org.uk/

*Mind*

Provides advice and support to empower anyone experiencing a mental health problem through 125 'Mind Services' in England and Wales.
*COVID-19 support.*
www.mind.org.uk

*MindEd*

> Funded by Health and the DfE, this is an online resource for all those interested in, or concerned about, the mental health of children and teenagers.
> *COVID-19 support.*
> www.minded.org.uk

*Mindfulness in School Project (MiSP)*

> The Project gives teachers the tools and training to be able to embed mindfulness in their schools.
> www.mindfulnessinschools.org

*Mind Up*

> A programme created by the Goldie Hawn Foundation, which aims to help children understand the neuroscience behind emotions.
> www.mindup.org

*National Association for Pastoral Care in Education (NAPCE)*

> Founded in 1982 to establish links between education professionals and allied agencies who have an interest in pastoral care and personal-social education and the welfare of students of all ages in schools.
> www.napce.org.uk

*Nurture Groups*

> These are in-school, teacher-led intervention groups that seek to replace missing earlier nurturing experiences.
> www.nurtureuk.org

*Partnership for Children*

> Partnership for Children is a UK-registered charity that helps children to be mentally and emotionally healthy.
> *COVID-19 advice.*
> www.partnershipforchildren.org.uk

*Place2Be*

> Place2Be is a children's mental health charity with over 25 years' experience working with pupils, families and staff in UK schools.
> *COVID-19 support.*
> www.place2be.org.uk

*Pooky Knightsmith*

> Mental health educator, speaker, author and advisor
> www.pookyknightsmith.com/

*Protective Behaviours*

> A safety awareness and resilience framework, which helps children to recognise when they feel stressed or unsafe.
> www.protectivebehaviours.org

*PSHE Association*

> Provides information and guidance for the delivery of PSHE curriculum from reception to Y13.
> www.pshe-association.org.uk

*Rebound Therapy*

> Rebound therapy is the phrase that describes a specific model of trampoline therapy.
> www.reboundtherapy.org

*Recovery Curriculum*

> Advice and guidance to support pupils as they return to school.
> www.recoverycurriculum.org.uk

*Restorative Justice*

> Restorative Justice allows victims of crime to communicate with the offender, often with the aim of a face to face meeting.
> www.restorativejustice.org.uk

*Rethink Mental Illness*

> Provide mental health services in England, for people living with mental illness and those who care for them.
> www.rethink.org

*Revised Children's Anxiety and Depression Scale (RCADS)*

> The Revised Child Anxiety and Depression Scale (RCADS) is a 47-item, youth self-report questionnaire.
> www.corc.uk.net

*Social and emotional aspects of learning (SEAL)*

> Social and emotional aspects of learning (SEAL), introduced in 2007, is a comprehensive, whole-school approach to promoting the social and emotional skills.
> https://assets.publishing.service.gov.uk/government/uploads/system/uploads/attachment_data/file/181718/DFE-RR049.pdf

*SHANARRI*

> The Children and Young People (Scotland) Act 2014, which includes key parts of the Getting it Right for Every Child approach

(GIRFEC), defines Child Wellbeing in terms of eight indicators of wellbeing.

www.gov.scot/policies/girfec/wellbeing-indicators-shanarri/

*shout 85258*

A confidential, 24/7 text-messaging support service for anyone who is struggling to cope.

www.giveusashout.org

*Solihull Approach*

The Solihull Approach aims to increase emotional health and wellbeing through both practitioners and parents.

www.solihullapproachparenting.com

*Strengths and Difficulties Questionnaire (SDQ)*

The Strengths and Difficulties Questionnaire (SDQ) is a brief behavioural screening questionnaire about 3 to 16-year-olds. It exists in several versions to meet the needs of researchers, clinicians and educationalists.

www.sdqinfo.org

*SWERL*

This is a knowledge-exchange programme, bringing together research and practitioner expertise to enhance and support the wellbeing and mental health of staff and pupils in schools. Based at University College, London.

www.ucl.ac.uk

*Talking therapies*

These are psychological treatments for mental and emotional problems like stress, anxiety and depression.

www.nhs.uk/conditions/stress-anxiety-depression/types-of-therapy/

*Thrive approach*

This is used in schools as a way of meeting pupils' emotional and social needs. Thrive-online is a recording system that goes with it. *COVID-19 support.*

www.thriveapproach.com

*Thrive framework/i-Thrive accelerator*

This is an alternative way of describing young people's mental health needs, using five needs-based groupings rather than four tiers. The i-Thrive accelerator is the implementation tool.

https://www.annafreud.org/mental-health-professionals/thrive-framework/

*Trauma informed schools (TIS)*

A trauma informed school is one that is able to support children and teenagers who suffer with trauma or mental health problems and whose troubled behaviour acts as a barrier to learning.
www.traumainformedschools.co.uk

*Time to Change*

A group that want to change the way to think and act about mental health. *COVID-19 support.*
www.time-to-change.org.uk

*Unconditional positive regard (UPR)*

UPR is unconditional acceptance, love or affection. The term is credited to the humanist psychologist Carl Rogers.

*YoungMinds*

YoungMinds work to prevent mental health illness from developing and to improve early intervention and care for children and young people living with a mental health problem.
*COVID-19 resources and advice.*
www.youngminds.org.uk

*YP-CORE Outcome Measure*

A CPD hub for those who have counselling or psychotherapy qualifications to develop their skills and knowledge further.
www.bacp.co.uk

*Zones of Regulation*

These are used as a means of helping children to gain impulse control (self-regulation). Emotions are seen in terms of four colours.
www.zonesofregulation.com

*The book ends with the poem by a student at Leamington LAMP, which was mentioned in Chapter 5.*

*Extract from 'Full Circle'*

Time flies so quick, been over a year
since I couldn't leave the house, too much to fear
Always looking round jumping at the slightest sound
People out to hurt me, knock me to the ground.

No longer under attack
I dont have to worry whose behind my back
My heads up, my hoods down
smile on my face walking to town

No more, running for the hills
standing tall with the world at my heels
no more hiding, I am revealed
taking control of all emotions I feel.

What a year, carrying this weight
struggled alone my heart full of hate
insomnia kicked in, I never slept
left me broken I cried and I wept

At my new school, I can now be myself
Self-prescription fixing my mental health
Just realised there's more to life than wealth
Started to make changes, help myself

Gone full circle, total reversal
No longer afraid, im over these hurdles
Ghosts from my past no longer haunt me
Inner strength is now the light that guides me

by J Flo

# Index